# "Failure" Is Written In Pencil

how to turn your failures into success

# David Ireland

PUBLISHING HOUSE

MONTCLAIR, NEW JERSEY

Published by IMPACT Publishing House
68 Church Street
Montclair, New Jersey, U.S.A. 07042
www.impactministry.org

ISBN 0-9627907-2-9
Printed in the United States of America
LC 00-100989

| **Library of Congress Cataloging-in Publishing Data** |
| --- |
| Ireland, David, 1961—<br>Failure Is Written In Pencil / David Ireland.<br>     p.            cm.<br>     Includes bibliographical references.<br>     ISBN 0-9627907-2-9<br>     1. Failure Is Written In Pencil—United States.<br>     I. Title.<br>       2000 |

# *Contents*

# *Acknowledgements*

Special thanks to Sylvia and Vincent Ireland, my parents, who taught me that failure is erasable—it's written in pencil.
This book is lovingly dedicated to their honor.

# INTRODUCTION

True success has a way of causing you to walk with your head held high and your shoulders squared. The sense of personal fulfillment makes you feel almost invincible. On the other hand, failure has a way of cutting to the core of your being, leaving you emotionally dejected. Like the dreaded AIDS virus to the body's bloodstream, failure attacks the immune system of the soul. A significant number of people walk around wounded and crippled to the idea of achieving their dreams because they have been infected with the failure virus. Consequently, failure must be combated aggressively and tactically. Failure will inevitably come knocking at your door. When it does, it should be met head-on with an adequate dose of spiritual penicillin—the strength you've derived from personal fulfillment.

Despite the moderate success I now enjoy as the senior pastor of a congregation of over two thousand members, a consultant to church leaders, and a busy itinerant speaker, I must admit that I don't have the Midas touch! Everything I touch doesn't instantly turn to gold. In fact, sometimes my best laid plans simply go up in smoke. I do, however, qualify to write a book on failure because of the victories I've earned through my failures and shortcomings. My failures became the back door to my successes.

At times, I feel as if I've earned a Ph.D. in failure with a minor in frequent mistakes! Let's be honest; who wants to read a book on failure, written by a master failure? Not I! And certainly not you! The mere fact that I have experienced failure does not automatically give me the credentials to cheer others on to victory. However, looking back over my failures, I can see how they led to my eventual triumph over disastrous defeats. Like footprints in the sand, they show where I have come from by the grace of God. They are the credentials that give me the authority to lead discouraged people to a place of wholeness, victory, and success. High achievers are people who simply get up after they fall down. It's not just getting up, however, that qualifies one as an achiever. It is what you discover and embrace while floundering on the floor that leads you to a newfound fulfillment in life.

No matter how much faith we have in a better tomorrow, human nature says, "Give me a success story; hope is what I need to hear. Show me how to get out of my hole." In other words, "How should I handle my failures?" is the $64,000 question. The key to conquering failure is to accept and understand that "God works in all things for the good of those who love him, who have been called according to his purpose" (Romans 8:28). This Scripture provides a clear sense of God's commitment to help you, despite the awkward predicament you may find yourself in.

I have three goals in mind for this book—three nuggets of wisdom I picked up while wrestling on the floor with failure. First, I want to encourage you. The antidote for failure is encouragement. Often, encouragement is not easily achieved. Have you ever been scratched where you don't itch? All of us have at one time or another. When my back is itching and I ask my wife to scratch it, she will invariably start scratching in a spot that isn't itching. I have the toughest time navigating her fingers to the area that needs the attention. Sometimes she just walks away in frustration because my navigational commands aren't getting her to the spot quickly enough! Other times I'm the one who walks away muttering and twisting because my back is still itching and she couldn't bring me relief. This book is written to scratch your itch by directing words of encouragement to the spot in your soul where help is needed.

Second, I want to present workable principles of failure management. Most of us have either done things or had things done to us that have left a bitter taste in our mouths. This book offers biblical solutions to overcoming past failures, outlined in a way that will release hope. Your potential will be clarified and your dreams will be realized by turning the failures of yesterday into the stepping stones of tomorrow's successes. The excitement of seeing God working in your life will grow.

Consider the time when Jacob was told by God's angel that his name would no longer be *Jacob*, but *Israel*. The characteristics of a deceiver, a heel-grabber, and a manipulator were all associated with the name *Jacob*. Yet Jacob saw the possibility of walking away from the failures of his past when God changed his name to *Israel,* meaning "a prince with God" (Genesis 32:22–32).

Third, my hope is to help you laugh at yourself. The shame and power of failure are broken when you can find humor in your past mistakes and bad judgments. Victory is realized when you understand that your personal worth is not based on what you do, what you have, or whom you are with—but on who you are.

I heard about an eight-year-old boy who brought home a report card filled with poor grades. His mother asked, "What have you to say about this?" The boy replied, "One thing is for sure, you know I ain't cheating!" Even this little boy could find a bright side to his failure.

As serious as life is, you must look for frequent opportunities to chuckle. Look for the silver lining in your cloud. This book is like chicken soup to a common cold. Don't be a bad patient! Follow the prescription to laugh, laugh, laugh! Even if this book does nothing but make you chuckle, it has accomplished its purpose.

# Chapter 1

# THE SPAGHETTI FACTORY

*When opportunity knocks, a grumbler*
*complains about the noise.*
*—Author Unknown*

For the first sixteen years of my life, things were quite normal. I grew up in a non-Christian household, where education was promoted as the primary answer to all the questions of life. As a result, I began college at age sixteen, with the intention of completing a doctorate degree by age twenty-five. Having completed my first degree in mechanical engineering at age twenty and my first master's degree in civil engineering at age twenty-two, I was well on my way. But eighteen months before completing graduate school, I became a Christian. That was the turning point. From that moment, all my plans for the future went topsy-turvy.

Six months before earning a master's degree in civil engineering, I began praying, "God, give me a job by graduation day." It was a very honest and simple prayer request, I thought. Two months later, I had no job offers. As a young Christian, I began praying, "God, if You give me a job by the end of May, I'll tithe my income." Two months after that, I still had no job offers. Since God had not responded to my earlier decision to give Him 10 percent of my future income, I thought He was holding out for more. So I began to sweeten the terms of my negotiations. I began praying, "God, if You give me a job in my field by graduation, I'll not only give 10 percent of my income to Your kingdom, but I'll kick in an additional 5 percent." Guess what? God still didn't respond to my monetary incentives. Don't you hate when God is silent, even in the midst of our concept of proper timing? It's as if He's snickering in heaven at our feeble attempts to alter His perfect plan. He knows that His plan will result in our rejoicing, but we, on the other hand, don't have a clue as to what's going on.

Before graduation day, I upped the ante to 20 percent. Still no job prospects appeared, despite my many interviews. A week after graduation, armed with a 3.5 grade point average from Stevens Institute of Technology (an excellent engineering school), the only job I could get was in a spaghetti factory. No, I wasn't hired as a mechanical or civil engineer to design a new addition to the plant or improve upon the efficiency of the existing machinery. I was hired as a temporary worker on the assembly line. My job was to package the company's spaghetti. No junior high, high school, college, or graduate education was required. All they wanted was someone with a pulse, who could follow rules and take orders from a belligerent, uneducated drill sergeant of a foreman.

My specific job was to stand on a thirty-foot metal platform and push spaghetti down a mechanical chute, where it would be packaged for wholesale distribution. Periodically, I'd hear my boss yelling up at me from the floor, "David, you're doing it the wrong way!" I thought to myself, "Here is a man with a third grade education, berating me in front of dozens of people." I interpreted this time in my life not simply as a trial, but as a huge failure.

At the end of the week, I walked out of there with a hefty paycheck of one hundred dollars. Glory to God! Yeah, right! Here I was, a twenty-two-year-old with a master's degree in engineering, trying not to get fired from a job on an assembly line in a spaghetti factory! Despite the psychological, spiritual, and emotional dilemma I was in, I still gave God my tithe. But because God didn't deliver the engineering job I had negotiated for in prayer, I didn't give the 20 percent I had promised prior to graduation.

After much prayer and fasting, I was able to secure another employment opportunity. This time I landed a job in a pizza factory. Looking back, it seems so funny. However, it wasn't at all funny at the time. I was experiencing severe disappointment and unmerciful discouragement. The new company manufactured frozen pizza. One day I was terribly hungry, but I had no money to buy lunch. All the workers on my shift were eating pizza in the cafeteria. And there I was, lusting after their food while claiming I was on a fast. About five minutes before our lunch hour was over, a co-worker said to me, "David, aren't you eating? The pizza is free to all employees." My eyes lit up like a Christmas tree when I heard the word "free." But just then, the bell rang to indicate that lunchtime was over. As my stomach growled from hunger, I vowed that the next day I would eat the largest pizza they had.

Before I could live out my promise, my employment agency assigned me to a better paying job at another factory, starting the very next day. This company manufactured plastic bottles that were dyed and labeled with the Clairol insignia. My first day at the plant, I walked over to where the engineers were working, only to find that I was in the wrong place. My work station was with the laborers whose job it was to pour boxes of plastic bottles into a mechanical chute, so that they could be imprinted with the appropriate labels. Oh, how I despised this time in my life! I was constantly haunted by thoughts that I was a first-class failure. I became so depressed and disillusioned in my walk with the Lord that I eventually withdrew from society. My pride about my educational accomplishments was being shattered right before my eyes, and there was nothing I could do about it. I was in the dealings of God, and I didn't like it one bit. Nonetheless, I continued to be faithful in my church attendance and tithing responsibilities.

On one particular day, the thought that I was a failure was beating me so hard that I just had to do something to alleviate the pressure. I decided to pray in my car during my lunch break at the bottling plant. Have you ever come to a point in prayer where you lose all concept of personal dignity? All of your emotional anguish and bitterness just wells up into a burst of ugly-faced weeping before the Lord. Charles Haddon Spurgeon, the great Baptist preacher, described this mournful state as "liquid prayers." My time of weeping became an intense period of intercession before the Lord. The Hebrew word for *intercession* is *paga*. It means "to meet with in order to converse; then, to make petition, especially to plead with a person." This prayer time was an official meeting to plead with God regarding my unbearable circumstances.

I remember crying out to God, "Please take this trial from me. I can't deal with failure any longer!" As my emotions subsided, I recall how God changed my heart as I was crying out to Him in utter desperation. This time I heard myself praying, "Lord, I will work in any factory and do anything You want me to do, as long as I'm in the center of Your will. If this is what it takes for me to become a man of God, I will do it." That afternoon, in the parking lot of a bottling plant, I became a man of God. Although I had been a Christian for about two years, I had not yet surrendered my will to God. The words of A. W. Tozer, the renowned author and preacher, rang true in my heart: "The whole man must make the decision before the heart can know any real satisfaction. God wants us all, and He will not rest till He gets us all. No part of the man will do."[1] God finally had all of me. He was now my Lord.

No, I didn't get an engineering job the next day. In fact, it was several months before I would start working as a civil engineer in an engineering consulting firm. Between the bottling plant and my first engineering job, I landed a job as a janitor for a major communications firm. This time, however, I had peace. I didn't envy others, nor did I care what others thought of me in my position. I knew that God had worked in my soul a sense of victory over the thoughts of fear of failure.

Each of us has a different definition of failure. However, we can all agree that failure is simply the realization that things are not going the way we intended. I hadn't planned, after graduating with excellent grades and receiving an all-expense-paid graduate fellowship, to work factory jobs. In my mind, there was no other conclusion to make: I was a failure.

Like a whirlwind meeting a house of cards, God totally demolished my plans. But that's what makes Him Lord. He really knows how to change your mind. Have you ever been going along, minding your own business, when you heard God say, "Hey, what do you think you're doing?" The question suggests that God is about to redirect your steps. And there's this sinking feeling that you may not understand or like the change—at least not initially. If you've submitted your life to God, you probably have learned that He wants to take full credit for making you, and that He isn't interested in sharing any of His glory with you or anyone else. God's ability to direct our steps, even through failure, is how He makes us totally pliable to His will. This is why the apostle Paul wrote, [27]"But God chose the foolish things of the world to shame the wise; God chose the weak things of the world to shame the strong. [28]He chose the lowly things of this world and the despised things—and the things that are not—to nullify the things that are, [29]so that no one may boast before him" (1 Corinthians 1:27–29).

## FAILURE IS RELATIVE

Everyone has a different definition of failure. One person's failure is another person's norm. Some children rejoice when they get a "C" on a math test, while others cry because a "C" to them spells failure. Once, at a meeting of church leaders from various denominations, we went around the room stating our personal prayer needs. One gentleman said, "Brothers and sisters, please pray about my personal finances. My private checking account has just dropped down to about $16,000." We all knew from the tears in his eyes and the trembling of his voice that this financial challenge was really causing him serious distress.

After he shared his prayer request, another brother jumped up and blurted out in a sarcastic tone, "You don't have a financial challenge! I have thirty dollars in my checking account, and I have the peace of God." At that point, we didn't know how to respond to our brother's prayer request. Some people laughed under their breath, while others assumed a posture for prayer. Remember that God is the same adviser of these two men, even though they held varying definitions of need. While one was unhappy but relatively wealthy, the other was at peace though not as prosperous. To the less prosperous man, $16,000 would have represented a major windfall, but to the other it was a point of crisis. Everyone has a different definition of what is a crisis, a need, or a failure.

## THE AMERICAN DREAM

Americans are enamored with success. Most don't even realize, however, that this desire for success is a form of idolatry. Although you don't see people physically bowing down and worshipping gold statues and other icons of materialistic wealth, the commitment of time, energy, and strength we make to this god is highly respected and often rewarded in our society. Because of its deceptive nature, success en-snares unsuspecting captives and anchors them to the here and now. Adherents of this life-style claim that eternity is too far away to think about or too unimportant to pay attention to right now. Most Americans crave this drug called "success" because it is presented to us as the key to fulfillment from the time we're old enough to point to a toy commercial and tell our parents, "I want that!" All the hoopla surrounding this supposed paradise—filled with material things and certificates of achievement—is so loud that the warning cries of its past victims are utterly drowned out.

John Bunyan, in his classic book *Pilgrim's Progress,* chose a character named Pliable to represent a type of personality common among people. Pliable's goal in life was constantly being redefined by his inability to reap the benefits of struggle. When he faced his first obstacle en route to the land of paradise, Pliable chose to turn around and go back home. He sadly asked the main character, Christian, "If we have had such a bad beginning, who knows what dangers we shall run into before the journey is over? If I get out of this with my life, you may possess that brave land alone for all I care."[2] At this, Pliable returned home and discontinued his search for the Celestial City. Pliable was swayed wherever life's turns appeared the easiest and least painful. He never established his own purpose or personal vision for his life.

Rather than addressing the real issues, modern society would likely tell Pliable that he suffers from attention deficit disorder. Today's prescription for his problem would be that he shouldn't feel guilty for his frequent distractions and dodging of pain. We'd tell him that he should just do the best he can. The problem with this therapy is twofold: First, it doesn't create a responsible, maturing character in Pliable. Second, it locks Pliable into the delusion that true success lies just over the next pain-free hilltop. Like fool's gold, painless distractions are glitters that lure the unsuspecting into the trappings of success as defined by society. This success promises substantial fulfillment, but cannot withstand the test of time, pressure, or trial by fire.

We all think we know the difference between true and false success. Yet how many times has a stretch limousine passed you on the road, and you've daydreamed about the famous person riding behind those smoked glass windows? "What would it be like to have a chauffeur drive me around in one of those fancy cars?" you wonder. As if perpetuating the delusion, your children jump gleefully around in the back seat of your four-door Chevy, trying to catch a glimpse of the movie star or wealthy tycoon who's riding off to some lofty place where only the ultra "successful" are welcomed. This fleeting glimpse of the land of "success" conveys to you and your children that prosperity is the panacea to all of life's ailments.

This erroneous definition of success whets an often insatiable appetite for material fulfillment. The word *appetite* comes from the Latin word *appetere,* which means "to strive after." The Hebrew definition of the word *appetite* includes the words "lust" and "desire." Hence, the word *appetite* indicates a mental, emotional, or physiological yearning for the item being craved.

Although acquiring material things is not wrong in and of itself, if this appetite remains unsatisfied, it will require that you devote even more time, energy, and strength to winning your next trophy of success. If you don't win the prize, however, this disloyal appetite will produce an overwhelming sense of failure. This incorrect view of success can be distracting and misleading. No alternatives are presented with this model. Make it—or live as a failure!

Several years ago, I hosted a leadership development conference in Kenya. During the evenings, after teaching and sharing all day, I usually retired to my hotel room to watch television and prepare for the next day's session. Invariably, during the commercial segments of the programs, an announcer would say, "You are watching your favorite Kenyan station." The first time it happened, I tried to change the station, hoping to find something of interest to watch during the commercials. I'll admit, I was channel surfing. I turned the dial to every number it had, but all I could find was a blank screen. Eventually, I wound up right back where I started. The voice came on again: "You are watching your favorite Kenyan station." I later learned that this was the *only* television station in Nukuru, Kenya. It *had* to be my favorite station! It was the only one. No other options were presented. Fortunately, we do have options when facing the challenges presented by failure.

## FAILURE THRIVES IN THE PRESENCE OF DOUBT

The most powerful, self-assured person can be deflated and broken by obsessive thoughts of failure. The fear of failure can also assault the unsuspecting before he even obtains his objectives. Many of us are so afraid of failure that we are paralyzed before embarking on a project. Our visions remain unfulfilled, safely tucked away in the recesses of our hearts and souls.

How you process apparent failure will either produce defeat or provide the energy needed to win the next battle. Immediately following the death of King Saul and his son Jonathan, David lamented, *"How the mighty have fallen! Tell it not in Gath, proclaim it not in the streets of Ashkelon"* (2 Samuel 1:19–20). There were two reasons David wrote this mournful song. First, the enemies of Israel would have rejoiced at the knowledge of the death of King Saul and Prince Jonathan. Second, the hearts of the people of Israel would have been exposed to fear and defeat had not the deaths of the reigning monarchs been properly reported. David was communicating—to his generation and ours—that there is a proper way to view failure and loss.

Consider the plight of a starving farmer who was paralyzed by fear. One day in July, the farmer sat in front of his shack, smoking his corncob pipe. Along came a stranger, who asked, "How's your cotton coming?"

"Ain't got none," was the answer. "Didn't plant none. 'Fraid of the boll weevil."

"Well, how's your corn?"

"Didn't plant none. 'Fraid o' drought."

"How about your potatoes?"

"Ain't got none. Scairt o' 'tater bugs."

The stranger finally asked, "Well, what did you plant?"

"Nothin'," answered the farmer. "I just played it safe."[3]

The fear of failure creates such a presence of doubt that reasonable and logical steps are abandoned. In the case of the farmer, he felt more comfortable playing it safe, even though he was unproductive and unsuccessful. He'd rather starve than risk planting a crop and having anything challenge it. Alas, the fear of failure captured yet another victim who heeded the delusion created by doubt!

Recently, I came across a simple poem about the contrast between doubt and faith.

> Doubt sees the obstacles
> Faith sees the way.
> Doubt sees the darkest night
> Faith sees the day.
> Doubt dreads to take a step
> Faith soars on high.

Doubt questions, "Who believes?"
Faith answers, "I."[4]


Fear of failure can cripple you before you can even get out of the starting gate. Your mind, moving at the speed of light, flashes thoughts of the worst possible outcome. When the angel of the Lord announced to Gideon, "Go in the strength you have and save Israel out of Midian's hand. Am I not sending you?" (Judges 6:14), Gideon's knowledge of Midian's superior military strength and the terrible state of affairs in Israel alarmed him. Keep in mind that he was threshing wheat in the safety of a winepress to hide it from the Midianite soldiers who were camping on Israel's land. Wheat threshing is an outdoor process. In Gideon's day, harvested grain was supposed to be spread out on a hard, level surface in the open air. When a tool called a sledge, made of heavy wooden boards, was dragged over the wheat, it tore the husks and the breeze would carry away the chaff, leaving the grains of wheat behind.

As soon as the angel voiced his statement, a flurry of questions rolled out of Gideon's mouth, revealing his fear of failure. His concerns ranged from "How do I know it is really God talking to me?" to "Am I going to die because I have seen the angel of the Lord face to face?" God had to calm Gideon down by giving him incremental steps to take. Gideon went from presenting a burnt offering, representing his desire for intimacy with God (Judges 6:18–22), to blowing a trumpet to summon his nation to follow him into battle against the Midianites (Judges 6:34–35). God helped Gideon overcome the fear of failure. Just the same, He can help us overcome the fear of failure and defuse the trauma of our past failures.

After completing a jail sentence, an ex-convict became a financially successful motivational speaker. He toured the circuit, making positive speeches to all that would attend. At one stop, a man angrily asked him, "How can you go around making these speeches and charging such an exorbitant fee when you can't even speak properly? In fact, you don't speak any better than I do."

The motivational speaker replied, "Which sounds better, 'I *is* rich or I *am* poor?'"

This illustration shows that your view of your failure makes all the difference in the world. A lot of people have failed in the same ways you have. Some are still crying over it, while others have used their failures as launching pads to personal fulfillment and great achievement.

When we look at ourselves, we see all of our inadequacies, short-comings, and reasons for failure. Yet in His infinite wisdom, God pays little attention to our fear-based reasoning. He knows that behind our phobias is a capacity for greatness. Therefore, He begins to work with us before we have a chance to vote in favor of—or against—His plans. And just as Gideon's fear was vanquished, our struggle with fear can be overcome if we trust in God's abilities.

Initially, the idea of completely trusting God can create apprehension and tension in our minds. But after we surrender to the tension, the results are peace of mind and spiritual harmony with God. Theodore E. Steinway, president of Steinway and Sons, explained that tension is the basis for the great harmony of his company's concert grand pianos. This great tension, created by 243 tightly drawn strings, exerts a pull of forty thousand pounds on the iron frame of a single Steinway piano.

Similarly, God creates tension in us by allowing us to confront our fears through trusting Him. Obedience to His dealings is a clear expression of faith, which translates heavenward as the melodious sound of your heart beating in harmony with God's.

# — Chapter 2 —

# THE BENEFITS
# OF FAILURE

*I've missed over 9,000 shots in my career.*
*I've lost over 300 games. Twenty-six times I*
*have been trusted to take the game-winning*
*shot and missed. I've failed in my life over*
*and over; that's why I succeed.*
—*Michael Jordan*

It's not hard to put your finger on the principles for successful living. The concepts aren't really complex, but living by them can be very challenging. Bypassing the basics is particularly tempting to those who think they'll become successful by their natural abilities and assets alone. How many people do you know who, after being heralded as prodigies destined for greatness, never amounted to much? History is replete with individuals who became world-changers, displaying astounding courage, character, and wisdom, without previous evidence of any talents and abilities that might cause them to become successful.

You never can tell who will rise to a high level of power, authority, or influence. The prophet Samuel was inspired by the Holy Spirit to pass over all of Jesse's sons in order to anoint David, a shepherd and the youngest of his brothers. Jesus, the greatest leader of all, was born in a barn in Bethlehem. Each time I speak to groups on the characteristics of greatness, it's as if I can hear the questions and doubts that run through people's minds: Can I ever be a real success? Is there some plan and purpose for my life that I have never even thought about? Will it require more faith, courage, dedication, and leadership ability than I possess? Do I really have what it takes?

Great people are not naturally born! Each one of us has the potential to be a uniquely successful person. That said, let me quickly point out one idea that we must immediately cast aside. It's the idea that if you've not yet been successful, you probably never will be. This is a tough one for many people, especially those who've gone through the pain of a serious failure or series of failures. The "I'll never win" mentality makes many people give up hope and quit dreaming. Successful people are often those who've risen to the challenge after they've experienced a series of devastating failures. In fact, when you look at those who have proven to be the greatest leaders of all, you'll find that most have had to deal with multiple failures. This characteristic is so common among great people that it seems failure has been an essential ingredient of their success.

My cousin Stewart and I are the same age. When we were both in seventh grade, I was placed in an "SP" class, which stood for "Special Pupils." As a budding connoisseur of educational accomplishments, I was immensely proud of my rank among my classmates. I was placed in "SP-2," the second highest of the four SP classes. Those of us in SP classes had not only bragging rights, but also the privilege of skipping eighth grade. "SP-2" was followed by "SP-3" and "SP-4," and then the regular Joes were placed in classes from the smartest to...well, you know.

The standard seventh-grade classes were ranked from 7-1 down to 7-21. Stewart had the double misfortune of being placed in class 7-15 and of being my cousin. I teased him mercilessly. Whenever he'd come into a room, I'd look at my watch and announce that it was 7:15, no matter what time of day it was. I'd do anything to work in a 7:15 dig to bug Stewart! My constant deriding grated on his nerves and undermined his self-esteem so badly that Stewart began to work hard and apply himself in school.

Today he is an executive-level manager for a telecommunications company and a doctoral candidate at a top engineering school. The other day he admitted to me that whenever he hears the number 7:15, he still winces a little and then chuckles. Recently, he was in an airport on a business trip, and he heard over the intercom, "This is the last call for flight 715." At this, all my childhood digs came rushing back to Stewart's memory, and he laughed to himself as he walked to his terminal. He has since told me that my teasing made him feel like a loser back then. But even in the face of browbeating defeat, Stewart turned his failure into success.

One of history's best examples of multiple-failures-to-greatness is Abraham Lincoln. He was considered an uneducated, uncouth backwoodsman, lacking the sophistication to lead a nation. His resumé was equally unimpressive. It was, in fact, a biography of repeated failures.

- He had a difficult childhood with less than one year of formal schooling.
- In 1831 he failed at business.
- He was defeated in his bid for the legislature in 1832.
- He failed in business again in 1833.
- He was elected to the legislature in 1834.
- His fiancée died in 1835.
- He was defeated for speaker of the house in 1838.
- He was defeated for elector in 1840.
- He was defeated for Congress in 1843.

- He was elected to Congress in 1846.
- He was defeated for Congress again in 1848.
- He was defeated for the Senate in 1855.
- He was defeated for vice president in 1856.
- He was defeated for the Senate in 1858.
- He was elected president in 1860.[1]

How many people do you think considered Lincoln a fool to run for the presidency after four straight defeats in the previous thirteen years? In contrast to public opinion back then, a recent poll revealed that Abraham Lincoln is considered the greatest of all the American presidents.

When a child fails at making the high school basketball team, it usually marks the end of his or her career. Michael Jordan failed to make his high school team, but is now considered one of the greatest basketball players of all time.

Albert Einstein was the greatest physicist of the modern era and probably the greatest of all time. Yet he was unable to speak fluently until he was nine years old. After being expelled from high school, he tried to enter the Federal Institute of Technology (FIT) in Zurich, Switzerland, but failed the entrance exam. Einstein went back to high school; two years later he passed the exam and was admitted to FIT. Not since Copernicus proved that the earth revolves around the sun has anyone changed the way we view the universe as Albert Einstein did.[2]

R. H. Macy, the founder of Macy's Department Store, failed in business seven times before his store in New York City became successful. Jack Hayford, one of the most respected and successful pastors in America, labored for years as the pastor of a fifty-member church before he became successful in his leadership of The Church On The Way in Van Nuys, California. He assumed the pastorate in Van Nuys when the church had a handful of members; presently the congregation numbers more than ten thousand members.

The ability to reach beyond failure is a common characteristic among those who are the very best at what they do. Rather than focusing on how many times you've failed, it's important to note the times when you didn't even make an attempt at success. Proverbs 24:16 teaches that though a righteous man may fall seven times, God still picks him up. Failure is undoubtedly the key to effective living. If you become an effective person, it will be because you have somehow been able to turn your failures into opportunities. Your effectiveness will be the result of your looking squarely at your failures and seeing them as a beneficial part of your journey.

## THE CROSSROADS OF FAILURE

With God all things are possible, even when you're trying to achieve success after repeated failures. There is no more dramatic example of this fact than the life of the apostle Peter. He was a unique character, a choleric with a capital "C" and a type-A personality with a capital "A." The choleric temperment, as personalities go, is more task-oriented than people-oriented, thinks he's usually right about his decisions, and tends to dominate his environment. Peter was bold but overly self-confident, ready to follow but impetuous, and quick to perceive but one who never understood as much as he thought he did. His leadership style could be described as "Ready, Fire, Aim!" God took Peter on a journey of failure to teach him the lessons of leadership. Peter needed to understand that leadership doesn't mean you have all the right answers. Rather, leadership means, among other things, that you know yourself.

If you've read the biblical account of Peter's primary bout with failure, you may have been surprised to see him fail so miserably. Remember that before Jesus was arrested, Peter drew his sword and was ready to fight. But when Jesus was facing death, Peter denied the Lord three times. It's hard to understand how he so quickly could have forgotten his pledge of allegiance to Christ, even amidst his disillusionment and discouragement. Peter failed in the most important test of his life. However, he was subsequently promoted to one of the greatest positions attainable on earth—a leader of the first church. Peter is proof positive that failure truly is the foundation of successful living.

Judas Iscariot probably had the same attitude of discouragement as did Peter during his assertions of denial. It appears that Judas was the first disciple to figure out that Jesus' earthly kingdom was not going to materialize. By Judas' estimation, Jesus was a failure. After hearing Jesus' promise that the disciples would sit on twelve thrones and judge Israel, and then seeing His reluctance to allow His followers to fight against the Roman soldiers, Judas was disappointed and disillusioned. At Jesus' invitation, Judas had left all he had to follow Him. Judas had planned to ride Jesus' coattails to a position of power. But at what appeared to be the opportune moment to seize power, Jesus turned away. The people would have made Him king, if only He had let them. Judas probably felt betrayed. In his mind, he was only betraying the betrayer.

People often conclude that they have been betrayed when the promises of God don't appear the way and at the time they had expected. This was the test of leadership Judas Iscariot faced. He was called as a disciple and probably anticipated being appointed as minister of finance in the new kingdom. As one of the twelve apostles, he was in position to become a great leader! But he took a wrong turn and was unable to recover from his failure. He eventually took his own life.

Simon Peter and Judas Iscariot were each at a crossroads in life. Every time we fail, we approach that same intersection. You may be at that place right now. Your failure may be eating you up. Your mistakes may be gnawing at your soul. What has transpired in your life may have caused you to view yourself negatively. You may have concluded that God will never do anything significant with you. You may be disappointed and disillusioned because things have not turned out as you expected. I want you to realize that failure is simply the back door to success.

Judas' failure destroyed him, while Peter's failure transformed him into an influential man. It's clear that our failures can have either a negative or a positive influence on us. Instead of being overcome with despair, we need to see the benefits our failures can bring.

## THE SEVEN BENEFITS OF FAILURE

Some people have a hard time dealing with losing. J. Neville Ward writes in *Five for Sorrow, Ten for Joy,* "Failure is as much a part of life as success is and by no means something in front of which one sits down and howls as though it is a scandal and a shame."[3] Recognizing the benefits of your failures will enable you to deal with them constructively. As a result, you'll be able to move on to the next challenge as a strong and effective person. Mike Markkula, vice chairman of Apple Computer, says, "Success does not breed success. It breeds failure. It is failure that breeds success."[4] There are many ways in which failures can be a help to you. Here are just a few.

### 1. Failure Positions You for Personal Change

Average people become great achievers by properly processing their failures. One of Thomas Edison's assistants questioned him about his bewildering number of failures—fifty thousand failed experiments—before he succeeded with a new storage battery. Edison exclaimed, "Results! Why, man, I have gotten a lot of results. I know fifty thousand things that won't work."[5]

We can learn and grow from our mistakes if we know how to correctly process the information. Sometimes our own pigheadedness is dressed up and disguised as persistence. A pigheaded person, in the face of failure, stubbornly keeps doing the same thing—only harder and without learning anything from the past mistakes. In his recent book, *Ambition: How We Manage Success and Failure Throughout Our Lives,* Gilbert Brim says this:

> After a losing episode, the most direct method of dealing with the achievement gap is to work harder, increasing the effort applied to the same actions. Sometimes this works. Sometimes it does not, especially when we try to force something to happen, like the child who unwittingly puts a key upside down into a lock and tries to get it all the way in by pushing harder and harder.[6]

It's easy to simply work harder; anyone can do it. However, great achievers learn from their failures so that they work smarter and more effectively.

Failing only helps you if you have the willingness to learn from it. Peter's three-fold denial was certainly not his first mistake. Peter failed in his understanding when, after beholding the transfigured Christ talking with Moses and Elijah, he suggested that tabernacles be erected for them, placing them on the same level with Christ. Peter failed in his faith when, walking on the water, he took his eyes off of Jesus. Peter failed when he drew his sword and cut off the ear of the high priest's servant at the time of Jesus' arrest. How many times did Jesus have to correct or rebuke Peter? It may have been hundreds of times. But it was the three-fold denial that taught Peter the lesson that created a personal change. One unmistakable point, however, is that Peter was willing to learn, even from his worst failures.

## 2. Failure Enables You to Have Compassion for Others Who Have Failed.

Failure will temper your tendency to be judgmental of the mistakes other people make. People want role models who are sensitive to their concerns. They want leaders who care about them and are empathetic to their needs. Failure is an important step in helping successful achievers become sensitive to others.

On their first missionary journey, Paul and Barnabas took along John Mark. The young John Mark was Barnabas' nephew. The journey, however, did not proceed without opposition. John Mark, overtaken by his fears, abandoned the trip at Paphos and went home to Jerusalem (Acts 12:13). When plans were being made for the second missionary journey, Barnabas again wanted John Mark to go along, but Paul would have nothing to do with this suggestion. The disagreement over the young deserter was so intense that Paul and Barnabas split company over it (Acts 15:36–41).

Barnabas took John Mark and traveled to Cyprus. But some time later John Mark retreated to Jerusalem again. There, he came in contact with Peter. What happened in Jerusalem is only a matter of speculation, but it seems that Peter, the apostle who had denied Christ three times, was able to identify with John Mark's shortcomings. What we know from church history is this: John Mark became the disciple of Peter. It is believed that he was with him in Rome right up to the point of Peter's execution. In his first epistle, Peter wrote, "She who is in Babylon, chosen together with you, sends you her greetings, and so does *my son* Mark" (1 Peter 5:13, emphasis added). Mark became Peter's closest assistant and recorded the apostle's recollections of Jesus. As a result, we enjoy today a book known as the gospel of Mark. Church historians also say that Mark was the first preacher sent to Alexandria, Egypt, to establish a church there—a church that later became one of the five major centers of Christianity during the first four centuries of the faith.[7]

The previously cocky Peter had been tempered by his own failures and was consequently understanding and receptive toward John Mark. He was also able to turn John Mark into one of the greatest, most productive men of the early church.

### 3. Failure Puts You in Touch With Your Frailties.

Jesus knew Peter better than Peter knew himself, and used failure to open the disciple's eyes. Peter's boldface denials, following his confident pledge of allegiance unto death, left the outspoken disciple broken and humbled. His shortcomings were evidenced dramatically and publicly. However, God's grace restored him. It is likely that this grace made such an indelible impression on Peter's soul that it changed him forever.

Understanding your weaknesses is more essential to great success than understanding your strengths. It is even more important than possessing great abilities. You can go out and hire other people for their abilities. But the self-awareness gained from personal failure produces leadership qualities that can be honed by you alone.

Great achievers also recognize that the strengths of others either are or can become greater than their own. They empower people with the freedom to be creative. By honoring the contributions of others, they create an environment in which people willingly accept responsibility without fear. These achievers characteristically assign priority to solving problems rather than assessing blame. They are secure enough to hire people smarter than themselves. They actively recruit with a goal of achieving the vision of the organization, and they willingly share the rewards of success. No manager or leader can exhibit these characteristics without first coming to grips with his or her limitations. A leader can often only understand these principles in the wake of personal failure.

### 4. Failure is Often an Opportunity in Disguise.

Great achievers are always alert to the new opportunities presented when they fail or when things don't go as planned.

After his Brooklyn butcher shop was robbed four times in one month during 1980, William Levine bought a bullet-proof vest. Other business owners asked him where they could get a vest like his. Levine began taking orders for vests to help these business owners feel more at ease. Today Levine is out of the meat business. He now works full-time as the president of Body Armour, International, a major supplier of bullet-proof vests.

African-American educator and innovator of agricultural sciences George Washington Carver graduated from Iowa State College of Agriculture and Mechanic Arts in 1894. Two years later, he became director of the Department of Agricultural Research at Booker T. Washington's Tuskegee Normal and Industrial Institute (now Tuskegee University) in Tuskegee, Alabama. There, he embarked upon an exhaustive series of experiments with peanuts. Carver wrote articles and gave numerous speeches to farmers about the need to rotate crops in order to keep from depleting the soil of all its nutrients. Only a few listened.

In 1902 the boll weevil migrated into Texas, devastating the cotton crop. Carver continually warned that the boll weevils were on their way and that Alabama farmers needed to be ready. If they planted peanuts and sweet potatoes, the spread of the boll weevil would be stopped. In addition, those crops would replenish the soil's nutrients. But nobody wanted to think about growing anything but cotton.

Just as Carver warned, the boll weevil chewed its way across Texas, Louisiana, and Mississippi, and finally arrived in Alabama. Just as Carver had predicted, in 1914 the Alabama crops were completely destroyed—except, that is, the peanut and sweet potato crops at Tuskegee Institute. People were now ready to listen. At Carver's suggestion, farmers began to plant peanuts. But although the boll weevil was stopped, Carver had made a mistake. There were so many peanuts available that the price of peanuts fell dramatically. Carver felt personally responsible for the financial ruin of everyone who had taken his advice. Everyone else blamed him too.

Carver retreated to his lab to avoid the faces of his students and friends. There, he cried out to God for wisdom. God answered and gave Carver the insight to begin experimenting with the horrendous surplus of peanuts his mistake had produced. His failure, and the subsequent research inspired by it, ultimately resulted in more than three hundred derivative products from peanuts.

The professor turned failure into a great opportunity. Within the next fifty years, peanuts became the sixth leading crop in the United States and the second largest in the South. Many dignitaries, including Franklin D. Roosevelt and Calvin Coolidge, visited Carver. He was befriended by Henry Ford and Mohandas Gandhi. He had job offers from all over the world, including one from Joseph Stalin. Thomas Edison offered him an annual salary of $100,000 to work with him. But Carver turned down all the offers and continued his work at Tuskegee. All of Carver's success was the result of his seizing the opportunity that his failure presented.

Your failure, too, could be an opportunity for success. Look at your life, determine where you have failed, and ask yourself the question, "How can I get up from this place of failure with something in my hand to be passionate and purpose-oriented about?"

### 5. Failure Helps You Guard Yourself.

Highly motivated people who are also blessed with great abilities often possess an arrogance and independence that gets them into trouble. They feel invincible and indestructible, and are inevitably snared by that attitude. In today's society, it is a cultural taboo to show any sign of weakness. Though this is especially true for men, both men and women work hard to guard their professional and/or social images from even the slightest appearance of weakness. Ironically, while their energy is spent guarding against the appearance of weakness, they unknowingly leave themselves vulnerable to the weakness itself.

Following Peter's hard-learned lesson on the pitfalls of arrogance, he never again boasted of what he would or would not do. After his failure, Peter understood and wisely managed his frailties and weaknesses. Successful people who have come to terms with their own weaknesses surround themselves with strong, confident individuals who can fortify their weak areas. Great leaders who understand their weaknesses are careful to build relationships that will provide protection, encouragement, and wise counsel. The depth and quality of your relationships have a great bearing on your level of success. It is counterproductive to hold yourself accountable to people of low standards or those too intimidated or too self-absorbed to confront your sensitive issues.

Failure presents a surefire way of getting in touch with your true self. All the warnings you previously ignored now sound like the wisdom of Solomon. Following an experience with failure, you guard your weak character traits the way a farmer guards his henhouse from a prowling fox. Many adulterous relationships and extramarital affairs would be prevented if couples were aware of the need to live guarded lives. Licensed psychologist and professional marriage counselor Williard Harley writes in his book *Surviving an Affair,* "The truth is that infidelity doesn't necessarily develop out of a bankrupt system of moral values. Instead, personal values change to accommodate the affair. What had been inconceivable prior to an affair can actually seem reasonable and even morally right after an affair. Many people who have always believed in being faithful in marriage find that their values do not protect them when they are faced with the temptation of an affair."[8]

Moral convictions alone won't protect you from making wrong choices. Past failures help you to maintain your alertness and guard against your weaknesses. The offensive action of guarding yourself will provide the needed deterrent against repeating a past failure. Being guarded does not mean acting cold, despondent, or emotionally detached from others. It simply speaks of living your life on the alert and placing silent alarm signals around your vulnerable areas. When a possible intrusion or moral breakdown is detected, the silent alarm warns your brain, saying, "Watch out! Red alert! Red Alert!" At this point, you become acutely aware of your weakness and take the appropriate steps to avoid the mishap.

## 6. Failure Makes You Dependent Upon God and His Power.

I'm not the least surprised that groups such as Narcotics Anonymous and Alcoholics Anonymous adopted the term "Higher Power" in their twelve-step recovery programs. These groups clearly acknowledge the need for God's help to break the power of a destructive, life-controlling substance over an addict's life. This philosophy of healing suggests that addicts are powerless in their ability to heal themselves and that a higher power is needed to set them free. Step three in the

Narcotics Anonymous recovery process is, "We made a decision to turn our will and our lives over to the care of God as we understood Him." The reasoning behind this step is clearly stated: "At times during our recovery, the decision to ask for God's help is our greatest source of strength and courage."[9] Although this group does not have any particular religious affiliation, it does acknowledge that true help lies in God's power and not in human origin.

The apostle Paul entreated the Lord three times to remove what he symbolically called his "thorn in the flesh." Here's what God said to Paul about the problem: "My grace is sufficient for you, for my power is made perfect in weakness." Consequently, Paul's conclusion was this: Therefore I will boast all the more gladly about my weaknesses, so that Christ's power may rest on me. That is why, for Christ's sake, I delight in weaknesses, in insults, in hardships, in persecutions, in difficulties. For when I am weak, then I am strong (2 Corinthians 12:9–10).

Like Paul, we all must acknowledge our need for God's power to overcome failure. There is a greater supply of God's grace—His might and power—when you and I become desperate for divine help. Failure creates a deep, emotional wound in the soul. Only God can provide the right remedy for our recovery. We all know of someone who cried out to God at a dark time in his life, and God rescued him.

I know a very precious couple who had to battle through a moral failure, and God walked them through the healing journey. Sure, there were professional, pastoral, and marital counselors involved in the process. But only God could heal some of the deep-rooted issues of their hearts. Their marriage survived because they relied on God's power rather than on their own. The wife had been unfaithful to her husband after their second wedding anniversary. She had become involved in a lesbian affair for several months. News of this sin devastated her husband. He felt betrayed on several levels. Naturally, he felt the betrayal of his wife. But he also felt that God had let him down because he had kept himself sexually pure until marriage. Time after time he asked the Lord, "God, why did this happen to me? I kept myself pure. I obeyed Your word for twenty-eight years, so why?"

Shrieks of this husband's grief could be heard throughout their town-house complex as he cried out to God for help. But in the end, I can honestly say that I saw God heal a man in a way that no pastoral counseling or other therapy could have. The God of the Bible stepped into this couple's world and showed Himself strong in the midst of their weakness. My only theological answer to the reason God unleashed His power at the husband's request was that the couple's failure created a desperation that compelled God to respond.

## 7. *Failure Helps You Identify Your Passion and Purpose.*

Failure helps you to see the really important things in life. When you fail, your dreams become clearer and your goals sharper. These dreams and goals are intrinsic to your existence. They are what you fought to maintain and protect from failure. Following your failure, you probably dedicated long periods of meditation and introspection to clarifying your values, passion, and purpose. Failure removes the unnecessary fluff from your life and crystallizes your reason for existing. Like a harsh taskmaster, it causes your heart to beat faster and faster for the fulfillment of your life's purpose. Oswald Chambers said, "Never let the sense of failure corrupt your new action."[10]  In other words, there is a definite benefit gained from failure, and future plans should not be dismissed because of a previous mishap. Most of us rush to get the memories and experiences of failure behind us. In our desire for a quick fix, we often overlook the benefits of failure. Like a wake-up call, failure arouses the true purpose for your life. We can greatly benefit from failure if we allow God to highlight the nuggets of failure's purpose, which are always hidden from the naked eye.

Charles Haddon Spurgeon once preached what in his judgment was one of his worst sermons. He stammered and floundered through it, and later felt that it had been a complete failure. He was greatly humiliated. When he went home, he fell on his knees and said, "Lord, God, Thou canst do something with nothing. Bless that poor sermon." He continued to utter that prayer all week long. He even woke up during the night and prayed that same prayer. He determined that the next Sunday he would redeem himself by preaching a great sermon. Sure enough, the next Sunday the sermon went off beautifully. At the close, the people crowded around and covered him with praise.

Spurgeon went home pleased with himself, saying, "I'll watch the results of those two sermons," and that night he slept like a baby. He later learned that the sermon he considered a failure resulted in forty-one conversions. From the sermon he thought was so magnificent, he learned that not a single soul was saved. The Spirit of God had chosen to use the so-called failure and not to use the other sermon.[11]

From Spurgeon's experience, we see that the Holy Spirit can take our mistakes and turn them into miracles. Investigate your life and determine if you have buried any failures that have the potential of becoming a gold mine of opportunity.

# — Chapter 3 —

# REJECT THE
# REJECTION

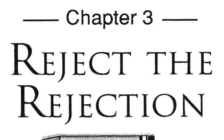

*A successful person is one who can lay a firm foundation*
*with the bricks that others throw at him.*
*—Author Unknown*

History is filled with men and women who rose from obscurity amidst insurmountable rejection, to make a significant contribution to society. These heroes became high achievers by overcoming the negative emotions, shameful treatment, and paralyzing effect that rejection produces. They showed a brand of courage and fortitude unmatched by others who faced similar circumstances. We all face failure and rejection at many junctures in our lives. Think about it. Even as infants, the first word we really began to understand was *no*. Though we didn't like hearing it, we understood in some way that we were being refused or that our infantile ideas were being rejected.

Granted, none of us will consistently hear affirming words or receive acceptance letters following every application we submit. Our world could not function justly if we never heard the word *no* in response to some of our requests. Even if you were created in sinless perfection, this would still be an imperfect world. Consequently, you must learn how to be on both the giving and receiving ends of rejection in order to function within society. No matter which end you most often find yourself on, handling rejection must become a skill you possess.

The bridge to your life's purpose is a bridge called "Failure and Rejection." But before you cross this bridge, the sign reads "Wrong Way." It's only after you cross the bridge and look back over your shoulder that the same sign will read "Failure and Rejection." And it's one and the same bridge! Your biggest failure will likely lead you to your life's purpose. Yet if you interpret "Failure and Rejection" as "Wrong Way," you may be inclined to make a U-turn and never cross the bridge to your destiny.

Noted author and church statesman Chuck Colson writes, "The real legacy of my life was my biggest failure—that I was an ex-convict. My greatest humiliation—being sent to prison—was the beginning of God's greatest use of my life; He chose the one experience in which I could not glory for His glory."[1]

Failing to reach your goals and encountering roadblocks en route to your purpose are things you must overcome if you are to become a high achiever. Failure holds on to its victims by stimulating feelings of rejection, which in turn shut you down from working at peak performance. General Colin Powell said, "There are no secrets to success: Don't waste time looking for them. Success is the result of perfection, hard work, learning from failure...."[2]

Because rejection is the child of failure, learning to handle rejection is an important skill to develop. Your response to rejection, however, must be in keeping with the laws of God (i.e., love, justice, and so forth). The chasm between failure and achievement is bridged by your positive response to rejection. Michael Jordan, the world's greatest basketball player, said, "When I got cut from the varsity team as a sophomore in high school, I learned something. I knew I never wanted to feel that bad again. I never wanted to have that taste in my mouth, that hole in my stomach. So I set a goal of becoming a starter on the varsity team."[3] A few reasonable questions to ask are: Where would Michael Jordan be today had he not experienced rejection? Would he have worked as hard to become a starter on the varsity basketball team if he hadn't previously failed? Would his destiny as a professional basketball superstar have been reached had he not won his earlier battle with rejection? I seriously doubt it! He did what you must do. He rejected the rejection!

## THE EFFECTS OF REJECTION

A person who becomes a high achiever has a dream inside his heart, and he refuses to let it die. *Webster's New World College Dictionary* defines the term *to reject* as "to refuse to take, agree to, accede to, use, or believe." A second definition of the verb *reject* is "to discard or throw out as worthless, useless, or substandard."[4] Hence, your immediate response to rejection comes in the form of confusion and uncertainty about the future. This feeling of despair creates a whirlwind of internal questions regarding your potential and the reality of achieving your dream.

Rejection causes you to rethink your life's purpose. It forces you to take a reality check. Rejection imposes upon you the idea that perhaps your dream is a fantasy, a wish, a delusion of grandeur, or a false hope. It nudges you to begin thinking in a smaller, more appeasing and substandard way. You begin to entertain and believe the notion that someone else's evaluation of your dream could be right. Then you may take this thought one step further. You start to seriously consider adopting someone else's dream for your life.

I've discovered over the years that whenever I let someone else dream for me, he always dreams too small. His limited definition of me, along with his tunnel-vision view of my skills and abilities, restricts me to a lower level of achievement. Such mediocrity goes against everything God has designed for us! The apostle Paul expressed God's dream for us by quoting the prophet Isaiah: "No eye has seen, no ear has heard, no mind has conceived what God has prepared for those who love him" (1 Corinthians 2:9). The Word of God instructs us to reject the rejection so that we can receive what God wants to accomplish in us by the Holy Spirit.

## REJECTION AFFECTS YOUR PERSPECTIVE

I have never seen anything that stifles a person's growth or self-esteem more than rejection. It wilts the flower of hope in your life. It brings a continual winter season to a person's world. Rejection is like a cancer to the soul. Two years ago, one of the elders in my congregation died of lung cancer. Gregory Thompson was a tremendous man of God who modeled the Christian life before all he came in contact with. But as he neared the end of his life, this dreaded disease suffocated him to the point where he could not breathe on his own. As the cancer progressed in his lungs, a respirator was eventually used to assist him in the breathing process. The cancer cells had caused fluid to fill his lungs and block the breathing passage. Week after week as I would offer words of encouragement and prayer for him and his family, the news of additional fluid draining into his lungs was reported. Finally, when he slipped into eternity, the comfort of being in heaven with Christ was his.

Rejection is cancer of the soul. The fluid of anger and resentment fills your perspective and prevents you from seeing life accurately. When rejection is not processed correctly, it causes anger and resentment to be formed against the person who rejected you, such as a parent, an employer, a friend, or your spouse. Rejection creates a narrow, antagonistic perspective in the heart of its victim. This faulty perspective can also be turned inward, causing the rejected person to blame himself for the failure. In either case, whether your blame comes from outside yourself or from inside, this ugly perspective injures you more than anyone else.

The first murder recorded in the Bible was committed by a man who became angry after rejection negatively affected his perspective of others. The account of this, recorded in Genesis chapter 4, shows God rejecting Cain's offering because it was not his best. The quality of the gift offered revealed that Cain's heart was not one of devotion and gratitude to God. In contrast, the Lord looked favorably on Cain's brother's gift because he presented the very best he had to give. Cain became angry with Abel and killed him without any provocation other than the rejected offering (Genesis 4:8). Cain's perspective of his brother became altered when God justifiably disliked his offering.

The meaning of the word *angry* in the biblical text is best compared to the kindling of a fire. In this case, Cain's anger burned uncontrollably for an extended period of time, even though God personally warned him of its danger (Genesis 4:6–7). Rather than dealing properly with God's disapproval of his gifts, Cain chose to allow the cancerous fluid of rejection to suffocate his perspective. His diseased perspective provoked him to plot and scheme to release the anger raging within. Abel's life was viciously taken away from him because of the cancerous perspective held by his brother, Cain.

43

## REJECTION AFFECTS YOUR SELF-ESTEEM

If it is not processed properly, rejection will adversely affect your self-esteem. When a person has been rejected in an area that's dear to him, the first painful step he often takes is to allow the rejection to bleed into the entirety of his life. This means that at the deepest part of his being, the question of value and personal worth is raised.

For example, we tend to connect an employment rejection with the rejection of our whole being. Rather than saying "I didn't get the job," we say "No one wants to hire me. I'm not employable." A termination notice can start many individuals spinning in an orbit of endless emotional depression. The dreaded termination letter provokes questions about your self-worth and personal marketability. You start wondering what others think about you. And how you judge the feelings of others begins to determine how you judge yourself.

Even members of the clergy, who labor tirelessly to pastor their congregations, are challenged with the issue of failure, largely because we operate in a success-driven culture. What the broader American society thinks about pastors and the importance of a large congregation causes many pastors to battle with depression and low self-esteem. A 1991 survey of pastors conducted by Fuller Institute of Church Growth indicates that approximately 70 percent of clergy in America say that their self-esteem was higher when they began serving in ministry than after several years of service. The arduous job of pleasing others can wear on a person's self–value—even a minister's.

The term *self-esteem* means "a confidence and satisfaction in oneself; self-respect; or self-confidence." From a psychological and clinical perspective, self-esteem measures the value you place on yourself. Your self-esteem can be raised or lowered by the affirmation you receive from significant people in your life. Therefore, if no one has deemed you worthy to receive verbal or material commendation, you walk around like a sponge, looking to soak up any type of praise you can get—whether from healthy or unhealthy sources. This is one of the primary reasons for teenage pregnancies, marital affairs, lust for power, and other attention-grabbing vices in our society. People are crying out for significance. Most individuals will look in any direction that offers significance or do anything that promises to lead them to it.

Rejection is the antithesis of significance. A rejected person believes intellectually and accepts emotionally that he doesn't qualify for significance. If God is not the first and most important source of your personal value, low self-esteem is sure to follow. Instead of suffering with this emotional ailment, cry out to God as did the psalmist: *"My soul is starved and hungry, ravenous!—insatiable for your nourishing commands"* (Psalm 119:20 *The Message*). During such times of emotional hunger, God will give you answers that will sustain you and heal your low self-esteem.

As a pastor, I have learned that my personal worth is not based upon my congregation's acceptance or rejection of me. It's based upon God's view of me. Period! The Old Testament character Job learned this valuable lesson during the most devastating time of his life. After Job lost all of his wealth and his children were suddenly killed, he concluded, *"Naked I came from my mother's womb, and naked I will depart. The LORD gave and the LORD has taken away; may the name of the LORD be praised"* (Job 1:21). Job realized that his value was not based on the abundance of his earthly possessions. In fact, he viewed all his wealth, including his family, as God's loan to him for a period of time. Job believed that God had a set period of time in which he was to provide the necessary care and love his family required. Therefore, when they were taken from him, Job was able to feel secure as a steward with the remainder of God's gifts. The biggest lesson Job learned is that he came into the world with nothing and would return to dust with the same amount of property—nothing. Job rejected the rejection of this world by focusing on spending eternity with God.

## YOUR REJECTION AFFECTS OTHERS

The story of my first bout with failure, which I shared in chapter 1, had devastating emotional effects on me, which I had to overcome. As a twenty-two-year-old, I had graduated with a master's degree in civil engineering, and the only job I could find was working as a minimum wage laborer in a spaghetti factory. I was not then—nor am I today—a lazy man. During my unemployment, I'd take any job—so long as it didn't compromise my personal relationship with Christ. For six months before graduation and six months afterwards, I must have sent out between two to three hundred resumés soliciting employment as a civil engineer. I received two to three hundred rejection letters. Other than my lack of work experience, there was no apparent reason for me to have been rejected by all these companies.

Do you know what it's like to open the mailbox every day to find three or four rejection letters? Some of the companies rejected me in a kind way. Others rejected me in a harsh, abrasive manner. Whatever the tone of the letter, it was a rejection just the same. Each day I became more and more disillusioned, depressed, and battle-fatigued.

During one of my sessions of self-pity, I thought, "Since my bachelor's degree is in mechanical engineering (rather than civil engineering), perhaps that's the employment route God wants me to take." So I quickly rewrote my resumé to emphasize this career path and mailed off about a hundred new resumés. I landed a few interviews, but eventually about a hundred rejection letters came back. Rejection became a part of my life. I started betting with myself on how many rejection letters I'd find in the mailbox each day. Some days I won, other days I lost. I was becoming cynical.

I don't want to paint the picture that every aspect of my life was horrible. God was meeting my daily needs in incredible ways. But although He was raining blessings in most areas of my life, there was a drought in the vocational area—the place where much of my significance was derived. I then inadvertently allowed this drought to negatively affect every other area of my life.

Little did I know that my personal battle with rejection was affecting other people. I slowly withdrew and eventually disconnected emotionally from my friends and family. All of their invitations to parties and social outings were refused. I even became distant and noncommunicative with my fiancée. I wasn't aware of how I was being perceived by the significant people in my life or of the effect I was having on them. My mood swings were drastic. One day I was pleasant, the next day I was cynical and sarcastic. The good that was happening to others was not met with any affirmation or excitement on my part. Rather, my friends could see that their good reports made me feel more rejected and worthless as a person. People stopped asking me, "Did you get a job in engineering yet?" Our conversations, by necessity, remained light and neutral.

No one knew how to approach me. If people did approach me, they didn't know what kind of response they'd get. Looking back, I praise God that I wasn't married and didn't have children at the time. The strain might have been too damaging to them. Imagine the countless number of people who are married with children, who struggle with this symptom of rejection. How do their families cope? What battle scars do these innocent victims wear daily? I know the answer. These are the men, women, boys, and girls who are your friends. They are the ones countless family therapists and pastors counsel. Some of them cry themselves to sleep at night because they don't know what to do about their family members who struggle with rejection. Others become workaholics because they'd rather not go home nightly and face the loved one struggling with rejection. Still others exhibit destructive behavior patterns in society or in the classroom. The rejection parents struggle with affects the behavior and self-esteem of their innocent children. We must reject the rejection in order to destroy its impact on our families and future generations.

One day following an emotionally heartrending time of prayer, I heard the Lord speak to my heart. He said, "David, if I asked you to work in a factory for the rest of your life, would you do it?"

I responded immediately, "Yes, Lord! If that is Your will for my life, I'll do it." Please realize that God was not saying that He was requiring me to do this. He just wanted to know if I would be willing to follow His leadership in every area of my life, no matter how unpleasant or misleading it might appear to be. It was at this juncture that my attitude about myself changed. In the midst of my emotional turmoil, I didn't have the words to explain what happened to me when I said "yes" to the Lord's question. But I knew that my perspective had changed.

In retrospect, I realize that the moment I answered God's question, I rejected the rejection of those hundreds of letters. My countenance changed. My attitude and demeanor toward my fiancée and friends became pleasant again. Some asked, "What engineering firm did you get a job with?"

I responded with joy and a big smile, "I'm still a worker at the spaghetti factory." They couldn't understand the reason for the change in my behavior. But it didn't matter. I understood. God gave me victory over my feelings of rejection. You alone determine the attitude you'll have when you face rejection and failure.

There are a number of other detrimental effects that rejection produces. These include self-hatred, an inordinate dependency on others, and little or no motivation toward personal growth. Rejection cuts deep into the core of human identity. It affects your choices of friends and a spouse, the clothing you wear, the type of car you drive, and even the house you live in since your outside is a reflection of your inside. The two are inseparable. The internal feelings of rejection are revealed externally by the actions you take on a daily basis. Therefore, you must reject the rejection.

## HOW TO REJECT THE REJECTION

Some of the greatest achievers in history were saddled with misfortunes but were able to overcome them by rejecting the rejection.

> Cripple him, and you have a Sir Walter Scott. Lock him in a prison cell, and you have a John Bunyan. Bury him in the snows of Valley Forge, and you have a George Washington. Raise him in abject poverty, and you have an Abraham Lincoln. Subject him to bitter religious prejudice, and you have a Benjamin Disraeli. Strike him down with infantile paralysis, and he becomes a Franklin D. Roosevelt. Burn him so severely in a schoolhouse fire that the doctors say he will never walk again, and you have a Glenn Cunningham, who set a world's record in 1934 for running a mile in 4 minutes, 6.7 seconds....Have him born of parents who survived a Nazi concentration camp, paralyze him from the waist down when he is four, and you have an incomparable concert violinist, Itzhak Perlman. Call him a slow learner, "retarded," and write him off as ineducable, and you have an Albert Einstein.[5]

The list of people who rejected the rejection of this world is end-less. Their testimonies cheer us on to overcome our own hurdles.

The question now remains: *How do you reject the rejection?* If others did it, you can too! My personal experience, along with that of many from history, reveals three general principles for rejecting the rejection. First, hard work must be set in motion. Second, a determination not to quit must be embraced. Third, the knowledge of when to change focus must be applied. These principles can help you achieve the results needed to fulfill God's purposes for your life. They are biblical in nature and origin. They do not discriminate. Anyone can benefit from them!

## *1. Reject the RejectionThrough Hard Work.*

The application of hard work—the kind that motivates you to-ward a passion for your dream—will help you defeat rejection. It's this kind of hard work that energizes you and becomes the wind that pro-pels you toward personal fulfillment. The difference between achiev-ers and failures is that achievers do what failures are too lazy to do. Hard work frightens failures. They would rather sulk about, rehashing their inadequacies, rather than throwing themselves headlong into the work of living. When I use the term hard work, I am not referring necessarily to your vocational responsibilities, nor am I excluding them. I am speaking of applying hard work to every area of your life—your dreams, occupational pursuits, and personal goals. Our lives are ex-tremely complex. Unfulfilled or unmined dreams will adversely im-pact significant areas of your life, even though they appear unrelated.

The world-renowned British novelist John Creasey has published 564 books. His first sale, however, didn't occur until after he had re-ceived 774 rejection letters from publishers. What do you think motivated him to continue believing in his dream? It certainly wasn't affirmation and encouragement from publishers or successful authors. He simply could not abandon the promise of realizing his dream, though he may have made countless attempts. His undying dream to become a published author was evidenced in his decision to keep working hard at it. He continued submitting book proposals to publishers, hoping that one day someone would accept his manuscript for publication.

How do you know that your dream is a worthwhile one? I've had to wrestle with this question for the greater part of my adult life. Many years ago I started writing down my thoughts with the small flicker of hope that they would someday evolve into a book. I wasn't looking for fame or notoriety. I was simply responding to a growing desire to write. I wasn't trained as a writer, nor did I have a childhood fantasy of becoming an author. I believed that what I was experiencing was a genuine burden placed on my heart by God. Although at times I tried to dismiss the idea of writing a publishable book, I couldn't escape the plan of God.

I felt like the professional football running back Deion Sanders. After he came to faith in Christ, he said, "As fast a runner as I am, yet I found out that I couldn't outrun God." I was trying to escape from obeying God in this area of my life. Writing a book was going to require too much work—too much hard work. When I finally completed by first book and forwarded the manuscript to several dozen publishers, I was faced with an equal number of rejection letters.

Rejection forced me to reevaluate my dreams and pursuits. I eventually decided to quit the writing business. But there was still a problem. God didn't agree with my decision, and He wouldn't leave me alone. I told Him, "I've quit! Let's just forget about this whole writing business." There's one thing about God that I don't like: He really believes He's God, and He thinks He knows what's best for me! Although I tried to convince Him otherwise, He stubbornly persisted in tormenting me with an undying desire to express myself in literary ways. So I kept knocking on publishers' doors until my first book, *Activating the Gifts of the Holy Spirit* (Whitaker House, 1997), was accepted and published. Quite obviously, I didn't stop at one book. I'm still plugging away with the hard work of pursuing God's complete will for my life. I rejected the rejection through hard work.

The opposite of hard work is procrastination. One reason you procrastinate is because the notion of hard work is either overwhelming or just too depressing. So you ease back on the living room sofa and remain a couch potato, mashed by rejection. Hard work requires determination, patience, and a focused outlook on life. It's a surefire way to overcome the obstacles rejection brings. Calvin Coolidge, the thirtieth president of the United States, said, "Nothing in the world can take the place of persistence. Talent will not; nothing is more common than unsuccessful men with talent. Genius will not; unrewarded genius is almost a proverb. Education will not; the world is full of educated derelicts. Persistence and determination alone are omnipotent. The slogan 'press on' has solved and always will solve the problems of the human race."[6]

## 2. Don't Quit Before You Start!

When you fear the worst, your own thoughts help to bring it about. Someone once wrote, "Fear is the wrong use of imagination. It is anticipating the worst, not the best, that can happen." Hence, many people quit before they get started in accomplishing their life's dream.

A salesman, driving on a lonely country road one dark and rainy night, had a flat tire. He opened the trunk and found he didn't have a lug wrench. The dim light from a farmhouse could be seen up the road. He set out on foot through the driving rain. Surely the farmer will have a lug wrench I can borrow, he thought. Of course, it was late at night—the farmer would be asleep in his warm, dry bed. Maybe he wouldn't answer the door. And even if he did, he'd be angry at being awakened in the middle of the night.

The salesman stumbled on. By now his shoes and clothing were soaked. Even if the farmer did answer his knock, he would probably shout something like "What's the big idea, waking me up at this hour?" This thought made the salesman angry. What right did that farmer have to refuse him the loan of a lug wrench? After all, here he was, stranded in the middle of nowhere, soaked to the skin. The farmer was a selfish clod—no doubt about that!

The salesman finally reached the house and banged loudly on the door. A voice called out, "Who is it?"

His face red with anger, the salesman called out, "You know good and well who it is. It's me! And you can keep your stupid lug wrench. I wouldn't borrow it now if you had the last one on earth!"[7]

The mind has a way of steering the entire body, just as the steering wheel dictates the direction of a car. The theological and philosophical thoughts you formulate in your mind tend to direct the moves you feel justified in taking. Therefore, it's important to know what's going on in your mind when failure takes place. Many questions that you may not regard as spiritual or theological in nature fall directly into these categories. Your understanding of the biblical doctrine of predestination, which simply means that God predetermines our destiny in conformity to His eternal plan, plays a significant role in shaping your thinking. An experience with failure may leave you saying "The reason I didn't succeed is that it wasn't God's will." If you're not a Christian, a bout with failure may leave you saying "Nothing good ever works out for me. I'm just not lucky!" In either case, you may quit before applying hard work to accomplish the task because of your faulty understanding of predestination. The difficulty or ease you experience in attaining a goal is not—nor can it be—indicative of the will of God.

There are numerous biblical examples of people who suffered major setbacks—even the loss of life—yet they were in the perfect will of God. Before Israel became a monarch state, everyone did what was right in his or her own eyes. During this state of lawlessness, a group of wicked men from the tribe of Benjamin raped a man's wife. Their sexual assault of her lasted throughout the night, and she died in the morning as a result. News of this heinous crime was brought to the other eleven tribes of Israel. When the Benjamites were asked to produce the guilty men so that capital punishment could be inflicted, they refused, and a war ensued.

The account of the battle and the events that caused it can be found in chapters 19 and 20 of Judges. Please keep in mind that the eleven tribes prayed to determine the will of God on three separate occasions (Judges 20:18, 23, and 27). Each time, God indicated that they were to fight against the army of Benjamin since the Benjamites were unwilling to see the guilty men brought to justice. The eleven tribes lost the first two battles against the Benjamites. The loss of life during these two encounters amounted to approximately forty thousand soldiers. These men were killed trying to obey what they believed was the revealed will of God. What was also remarkable was that Israel's army consisted of four hundred thousand men (Judges 20:2), while the Benjamites had a mere 26,700 troops.

What an incredible difference in manpower, not to mention Israel's moral cause. The men of Israel were fighting for a righteous cause, and God had sanctioned their actions with His blessing. They were in the right; they were operating in the will of God. Yet they suffered two significant losses and the death of forty thousand soldiers before experiencing victory. If the Israelites' thinking had been based on a faulty theological notion—namely, that all losses meant that they were outside of God's will—ultimate victory would never have been achieved. Similarly, if the Israelites had thought, "Difficulty or an excessive length of time in achieving success means we're outside of the will of God," they would have allowed this faulty definition of predestination to hinder them from gaining victory over the Benjamites.

The doctrine of predestination teaches that God has foreordained all things. It refers to the reality that He has sealed everyone to a specific destiny and fate, even before he or she was created. Predestination encompasses three areas of God's knowledge. First, He knows the worst about us. Second, He knows the best about us. Third, God knows what He is going to make of us. New Testament scholar James Montgomery Boice writes, "[God] knows the end we have been made for and he is most certainly going to bring us to it in his proper time."[8]

Although this doctrine reflects biblical and orthodox Christian teaching, it must be realized that God's ultimate plan for you centers on the person of Christ. The real meaning of life is not about your personal, earthly ambitions—the very things that cause you to panic if you don't see them occurring right before your eyes. Romans 8:29 tells us, *"For those God foreknew he also predestined to be conformed to the likeness of his Son, that he might be the firstborn among many brothers."* From God's viewpoint, predestination ultimately focuses upon His orchestration of your life to cause you to accept and live daily for Jesus Christ. Your earthly plans flow out of this heavenly plan. This is why Jesus said, *"But seek first his kingdom and his righteousness, and all these things will be given to you as well"* (Matthew 6:33). The security of your personal dreams is connected with a divine, foreordained plan, which is fail-proof. If you wholeheartedly pursue the kingdom of God, one definite by-product will be the accomplishment of your earthly plans. Don't quit before you start! God will see you through all the curves and bends in the maze of life as you keep your eyes focused on serving Christ.

### 3. *Know When to Quit and Set a New Focus.*

Sometimes we focus so resolutely on a goal that objectivity goes out the window. A key to success is maintaining enough emotional distance from your vision or goal that you can abruptly quit and set a new focus if the current situation is definitely not working.

Many years ago my wife and I were renting a house with a two-year option to purchase. We loved this gorgeous split-level home—its architectural charm was irresistible. The seller gave us a purchasing incentive at the onset of the lease. Each month, a portion of our rent would be credited toward a down payment, if we decided to exercise our option to buy the house within twenty-four months. We were thrilled. Everything seemed so foolproof; it felt so much like the will of God.

At the end of the twenty-third month, we began the paperwork to purchase the home. But no matter how much we tried, we could not secure a mortgage. Our down payment was in place, and our credit history was exemplary. On paper, there was no reason why we should have been denied a mortgage, but repeatedly we were. Our failure to secure a mortgage made us begin to rethink whether or not our "dream home" was in fact our dream home.

After much dialogue, prayer, and reevaluation, we abandoned the idea of buying that house and set a new plan in motion. Within a month, we were able to find another house that far exceeded the beauty, charm, and location of the first. Although the second house was far more expensive, we were able to negotiate a sale price that was lower than that of the first. We were also able to be approved for a mortgage at a lower interest rate. Our failure had caused us to quit pursuing a goal that was not working and set a new focus.

During that time, our church also changed locations, and the new site of worship was just twelve minutes by car from our new house. The lesson I learned was that failure is a teacher and a guide. Listen closely, and you'll find your ultimate destiny.

All high achievers know when to quit and begin establishing a new focus. If you're in a war and you run out of bullets, it's time to seek terms of peace. And you'd better know how to communicate that you want peace—not the fact that you're out of bullets. Don't say anything about your lack of ammunition. Focus on your newfound goal—namely, the mutual need for peace. I'm not by any means advocating fickleness. But in order to reject the rejections of this world, you must be certain that you're headed in the right direction. What's the use of driving at a hundred miles per hour, only to find out that you're going the wrong way?

I once heard a minister share a story about an American missionary sent to Africa. Over time, this missionary became depressed about his choice of service to God and his inability to succeed on the mission field. When a friend came to visit, he couldn't help but comment on his sadness as a missionary. His friend said, "If you had your choice of vocation, what would you like to do?"

The missionary replied, "I would love to go back to the States and sell hot dogs. I always wanted to open up my own hot dog business."

The friend said, "What's stopping you? Go!"

The missionary said, "I feel if I go, I'll be letting God down."

"Go," declared his friend.

So the missionary resigned from his post and went back to America. After a short time, his new business became extremely successful. Over the years he became a multimillionaire and was able to support missions by giving hundreds of thousands of dollars annually. This newfound success was a direct result of one man's courage to reject the rejection that failure brings and to set a new focus. Achievers are not perfect people. They are simply men and women who have made a commitment to get up from the ground after being beaten down by failure and rejection.

In 1902, the poetry editor of *The Atlantic Monthly* returned a sheaf of poems to a twenty-eight-year-old poet with this curt note: "Our magazine has no room for your vigorous verse." The poet was Robert Frost, who rejected the rejection. In 1905, the University of Bern turned down a Ph.D. dissertation as being irrelevant and fanciful. The young physics student who wrote the dissertation was Albert Einstein, who rejected the rejection. In 1894, the rhetoric teacher at Harrow in England wrote on a sixteen-year-old's report card, "a conspicuous lack of success." The sixteen-year-old was Winston Churchill, who rejected the rejection.[9]

It's your turn to enter the sacred halls of history by rejecting your rejection.

# — Chapter 4 —

# WHAT ARE YOU HOLDING ON TO?

*Failure is the opportunity to begin again, more intelligently.*
*—Henry Ford*

Have you ever noticed the unusual behavior of the cartoon character Linus? He's one of Charlie Brown's friends in the "Peanuts" comic strip. One of Linus' most notable characteristics is his tendency to carry an old blanket wherever he goes. No matter what the occasion, be it a friendly game of baseball or a day at school, Linus holds this rumpled blanket close to his side. Apparently, it provides him with some sort of emotional support. In a way, Linus represents many people today, who cuddle other strange security blankets.

For the most part, people who have experienced failure have been stripped of almost all of their valuables, both tangible and intangible. Or so you would think. I have met people who are in the midst of terrible failures, yet they won't let go of their blankets. These blankets are providing them with a sense of security, albeit a false one. What such a person doesn't see is that his blanket is caught in the door that is meant to close off his past failure. Unbeknownst to him, the blanket is extending the trial unnecessarily. His need to be in control is so great that it outweighs proper judgment and sound reasoning.

With each person, the blanket is different. For one person, the blanket is a destructive relationship that renders him consistently outside of the will of God. For another, it's an expensive life-style that should be downscaled to one that is more consistent with her income. For another, it could be a job that is clearly contrary to his gifting or life purpose.

No matter what the situation, the security blanket represents a last ditch effort to take charge of your life, despite the negative repercussions. Behind the struggle to let go of the blanket is pride. Pride is the protective layer you construct so that your failure doesn't cause you any further embarrassment. Pride is the natural response that pushes you to create the illusion that everything is okay, when it really is not. Failure gets you into trouble, but pride keeps you there. Pride distracts. Pride gives you a false sense of autonomy and a false sense of strength. It keeps you focused in the wrong direction for the wrong reasons. Pride makes you want to sink your heels into the turf and defend beyond reason. It is the one last strand of authority and self-determination that can be displayed with true grit. Nonetheless, as the Bible says, pride goes before a fall (Proverbs 16:18).

A crowd watched a peacock spread its tail and show its dazzling plumage one sunny day at the zoo. The bird drew oohs and ahs from the people as it strutted regally about its pen. Then a dullish brown duck waddled between the peacock and the crowd. The peacock became angry and drove the duck back, into a nearby pond. In his rage, the peacock closed his tail like a fan, and the bird looked ugly to the crowd of onlookers. Just then, the duck began swimming and diving gracefully in the pond and no longer looked unattractive. The onlookers, who had been singing the praises of the peacock, now loved the duck.

The moral of this little story is that the peacock's pride caused him to become distracted, and his true beauty was no longer evident to the crowd. When your pride rears its ugly head, it will divert your thoughts away from the real, foundational issues and onto areas that bring a warped sense of self-preservation.

Failure is a part of life. Everyone knows that failure exists and can strike at any time. It is best to be prepared to counteract its effects through wisdom. Life has its unusual, unexpected turns for us all. Who is wise or perceptive enough to predict when these dilemmas will surface? No one but God.

Prepare to live your life in such a way that you are not caught off guard. Once you are trained to handle the weapons that fight failure, your life will become more fulfilling. I am not suggesting that you walk around in paranoia, looking over your shoulder every five minutes to see if something bad is about to happen. Rather, the most wholesome approach is to have a strategy in place in the event that a failure does occur. This preparation is achievable by living in a principle-centered way. You should build specific principles into your life that can reduce failure's sting, ward off unnecessary attacks, and even manage any predicaments that are inescapable.

I've learned two such failure-management principles from my own bouts with failure. These are easy to adopt and cultivate as natural habits for anyone. First, ultimate living is walking in total obedience to God's commandments and expectations for your life. Most of the attacks of failure can be avoided through an obedient lifestyle. Second, failure occurs when you're not focused on serving God. To failure-proof your life in the best possible way, live as a servant of God. Once adopted, these failure-management principles will guide you through the storms of life without getting you shipwrecked.

## Principle #1: Obedience Is Ultimate Living

One day while walking down the street, a highly successful executive was hit by a bus and died. She arrived in heaven, where she was met at the pearly gates by Peter himself. "Welcome to heaven," said Peter. "Before you get settled in though, it seems we have a problem. You see, strangely enough, we've never once had an executive make it this far, and we're not really sure what to do with you."

"No problem. Just let me in," said the woman.

"Well, I'd like to, but I have orders. What we're going to do is let you have a day in hell and a day in heaven, and then you can choose whichever one you want to spend eternity in," said Peter.

"Actually, I think I've made up my mind. I prefer to stay in heaven," said the woman.

"Sorry," said Peter, "we have rules." And with that, he put the executive on an elevator and it went down, down, down to hell.

When the door opened, she found herself stepping out on the putting green of a beautiful golf course. In the distance there was a country club, and standing in front of her were all her friends—fellow executives with whom she had worked. They ran up and kissed her on both cheeks, and they talked about old times. They all played a round of golf, and that evening they went to the country club, where she enjoyed an excellent steak and lobster dinner. She met the devil, who was a really nice guy (kind of cute), and she had a great time telling jokes and dancing. She was having such a good time that before she knew it, it was time to leave. Everyone shook her hand and waved good-bye as she got on the elevator.

The elevator went up, up, up, and opened at the pearly gates, where the woman found Peter waiting for her. "Now it's time to spend a day in heaven," he said. So she spent the next twenty-four hours lounging around on clouds, playing the harp, and singing. She had a great time. Before she knew it, her twenty-four hours were up. Peter came and got her.

"So, you've spent a day in hell and a day in heaven. Now you must choose your eternity," he said.

The woman paused for a second and replied, "Well, I never thought I'd say this," she said. "I mean, heaven has been really great and all, but I think I had a better time in hell." So Peter escorted her to the elevator, and again she went down, down, down to hell.

When the elevator door opened, she found herself standing in a desolate wasteland covered with garbage and filth. She saw her friends dressed in rags, and they were picking up the garbage and putting it in sacks. The devil came up to her and put his arm around her. "I don't understand," stammered the woman. "Yesterday I was here, and there was a golf course and a country club. We ate lobster and danced and had a great time. Now there is only a wasteland of garbage, and all my friends look miserable."

The devil looked at her and smiled. "Yesterday we were recruiting you; today you're staff."

There are times when disobedience looks more enjoyable than obedience. The allure of unrestrained living or a lack of moral authority can really put you at risk to temptation. If you're not committed to living obediently before the Lord, before you know it, you'll be saying, "Hell isn't so bad after all." There are serious consequences for disobedient living, however.

No one wants to lose property or autonomy, particularly after working hard to obtain them. In God's infinite wisdom, however, our failures can be given to Him as an act of worship. True worship is a life-style of obedience to the revealed will of God. Mankind was created for God's pleasure. This divine enjoyment cannot be achieved when you hold on to things other than God. If you're not careful, your possessions can become objects of idol worship. Things have a way of getting between you and God. I'm not saying that God designed your failure to bring you close to Him. God does not use wicked, despotic, or devilish tactics to instruct or correct His children.

But whenever necessary, God knows how to discipline you in righteous ways (Hebrews 12:5–6). God is extremely resourceful, and He uses our failures to get us back on track, in true devotion to Him. Failure creates in us a fuller understanding of our values and priorities. It was David's moral failure with Bathsheba that became the catalyst leading him to rededicate himself to God. Psalm 51 captures David's heart cry of repentance. By the time he composed this psalm, David had finally become ready to obey God completely. Verse 17 conveys this sentiment: *"The sacrifices of God are a broken spirit; a broken and contrite heart, O God, you will not despise."*

A broken spirit speaks of a flexible heart, ready to be formed into whatever its master desires. No more rebellion, no more rejection, no more resistance or defiance. The fight is over. Charles Haddon Spurgeon wrote, "'A broken heart' is an expression implying deep sorrow, embittering the very life; it carries in it the idea of all but killing anguish in that region which is so vital as to be the very source of life."[1] Personal failure had broken the constant struggle of insurrection against God in David's soul. Israel's mighty king had finally surrendered totally to Jehovah. David saw the error of his ways because of the clarity of perspective his failure brought. The trail of destruction, which he created by his disobedience, was proof positive that his soul needed to be tamed. And, oh what a sweet fragrance his offering of a contrite heart produced in the nostrils of God.

## *You Need to Learn Your Lesson*

When I was six or seven years old, I used to tease my younger brother mercilessly. "Why not?" I thought. He was a year younger than I, so he was fair game. One morning I started bothering Norman for no particular reason other than that it was a new day. Well, he started crying loudly. My grandaunt, who was watching us for several months while our parents were overseas, heard my brother crying and came to his aid. He told her that I was hitting him, and that was all it took to start her chasing me. Aunt Edith was in her late sixties, and I was an agile, mischievous little boy who was always looking for a good time, especially at the expense of others. Since I was much faster than Aunt Edith, I decided to have some fun with her.

As she chased me through the house and outside, I ran slow enough to make her feel as if she was going to catch me. I kept my back about an arm's length from her to give her a sense of hope. Finally I tired of the game and ran to an area of the yard where I could climb a small tree and be out of her reach. After I scooted up the tree, I sat on a branch that was just high enough off the ground to make her think she could hit me with the broomstick she found lying in the backyard. No matter how high she jumped, I was safely out of reach by about two or three inches. Like a defeated warrior, she walked away without saying a word. Later that day, I came down from the tree and tried to act as normal as possible. Norman and I played together and ate the lunch Aunt Edith had prepared. Everything was going well, I thought.

After our dinner, baths, and a bedtime story, Aunt Edith tucked Norman and me into bed. There was no mention of the morning incident by Aunt Edith or Norman. I certainly wasn't going to bring it up. In my mind, everything had been forgotten, and my innocent sport with my grandaunt was behind us. However, about an hour into sleep, the lashes of a belt against my backside awakened me abruptly. As Aunt Edith spanked me, she punctuated each blow with an admonishment not to tease Norman anymore. I didn't hear every word from under the barrage of lashes from the belt, but the message was loud and clear. I learned my lesson. I stopped teasing my brother.

To achieve this state of obedience in your life, God must discipline you at times. As I previously stated, God does not use demonic methods to instruct or punish His children, no matter how inattentive or disobedient they are. However, He has a divine method of spanking that can grab our attention pronto. And He's not afraid to use it on any of His children.

## God Knows How to Dole Out Discipline

Since God delights in a broken and contrite heart, the place of obedience begins with submission. Failure should be our teacher, not our undertaker. Failure is delay, not defeat. It is a temporary stop on the way to our purpose. Failure is not a dead-end street. Disobedience is the blind alley ending at a roadblock. Failure is the back door to success. The lessons that your schoolmaster—failure—teaches must be learned quickly and thoroughly. If not, the class will be repeated until a passing grade is earned. No matter how you look at the crisis, you must learn the lesson in order to graduate. The problem is not your experience with failure; it's your unwillingness to learn the lesson it teaches.

God deals with us as my Aunt Edith dealt with me. He maximizes the quality of instruction by choosing the proper timing. The author of Hebrews wrote, [5] "And you have forgotten that word of encouragement that addresses you as sons: 'My son, do not make light of the Lord's discipline, and do not lose heart when he rebukes you, [6]because the Lord disciplines those he loves, and he punishes everyone he accepts as a son.' ⁷Endure hardship as discipline; God is treating you as sons" (Hebrews 12:5–7).

Three levels of painful instruction are used by God to bring adjustment and change in the behavior of His children. During every stage, the Father warns us to not lose heart when we are rebuked because He loves us. *Rebuke* means "to convict; to prove one in the wrong and thus to shame him." God brings out hidden flaws in our behavior that may not have been previously detectable to us. He does this so that we can make amends.

The mildest level of correction is expressed by the Greek word *nouthesia,* which is translated in the New Testament as "warning," "admonition," and "exhortation" (1 Corinthians 10:11; Ephesians 6:4; Titus 3:10 KJV). God uses this first method of instruction to modify our behavior through words of encouragement or reproof. His purpose here is to gently assist you in correcting your behavior by appealing to your conscience, will, and reasoning faculties. No actions are taken at this point because God wants to see whether His words of warning will suffice.

In many cases mere words won't bring about the needed reform. God then increases the method of correction to a second level, which is a stronger reprimand called *discipline.* The word *discipline* in Hebrews 12:5 is the Greek word *paideia,* which means "instruction by deed." Although God continues to appeal to the conscience, will, and reasoning faculties at this stage, His methods are stronger and longer lasting in a disciplinary sense. God wants to see our thinking and behavior turned around. The Greek scholar Kenneth Wuest comments on this word *discipline,* writing:

> It speaks also of whatever in adults cultivates the soul, especially by correcting mistakes and curbing passions. It

speaks also of instruction which aims at the increase of virtue. The word does not have in it the idea of punishment, but of corrective measures which will eliminate evil in the life and encourage the good.[2]

Level Two chastening is discipline by training. Since in the previous level words alone did not cause lasting change, God resorts to instructing us by deed. Our private issues have now been brought public. God's gentle conversations proved to be meaningless in effecting change in our behavior. Now physical actions are taken to move us onto the appropriate moral and behavioral path. Although Level Two corrections can be painful, take heart! Things get worse at Level Three.

If you continue in your stubborn attitude toward God's attempts to adjust your behavior, Level Three training is released into your life. This final level is distinguished from the first two stages by the word *kolasis*. This Greek word is translated into the English word *punishment* (Matthew 25:46). *Webster's New World College Dictionary* defines punishment as "a penalty imposed on an offender for a crime or wrongdoing."[3] This definition captures the essence of penal infliction but does not convey the biblical meaning of the word.

Greek scholar Spiros Zodhiates provides a more comprehensive definition. He writes that punishment is penal infliction that "satisfies the inflicter's sense of outraged justice in defending his own honor or that of the violated law."[4] God's outrage, initiated by your behavior and willful defiance of His law, moves Him to use penal retribution as the means of correction. Although this definition does not directly address the inflicted person's need to improve his behavior, most often his conduct will take a 180-degree turn. God is concerned about your behavior, but His anger is provoked because of your repeated actions of defiance. In other words, God is taking you out to the woodshed for a good thrashing.

An example of Level Three discipline was put on the worldwide stage in 1998 with the revelation of President Bill Clinton's extramarital affair with the former White House intern Monica Lewinsky. Knowing how the Bible describes the nature of God, I'm certain that He gave numerous warnings to both parties in this affair. Evidence of this can be seen on the part of Monica Lewinsky, who confided in another person regarding her frustrations about the affair. President Clinton was warned when his previous infidelities were made public. At the time of his affair with Lewinsky, he was already embroiled in a legal battle over his alleged sexual harassment of another woman.

Such spankings are painful and sobering. When God takes you out to the woodshed for a private spanking, it becomes public knowledge that the Father is displeased with you. Your inability to govern your personal actions and choices has resulted in your public humiliation. It's embarrassing when God has thwarted your life's plans or when the doors of opportunity have closed, one after the other. It's as if God's prior approvals have been reversed into firm disapproval. Divine restraint is uncomfortable and tight-fitting. But remember, God is disciplining you in order to get the appropriate responses.

## Are You Ready to Listen?

God is moved by love, even when it comes to doling out discipline. This is because He doesn't want to see you self-destruct or remain in the clutches of failure as a result of your own disobedience. However, failure can have a way of making you defiant. You may become defiant against God's plans, against sound judgment, or against the sober advice of the sages in your life. What you refuse to see is that your inability to listen to and appropriately respond to the conditions around you may be the very reason for your demise. Solomon described this kind of stubbornness with these words: *"How I hated discipline! How my heart spurned correction"* (Proverbs 5:12)!

Learning our lessons is a form of failure management. Everything in life must be managed—even our failures! Management means to provide the care and attention a specific area may require due to its inability to be governed by itself. Just as a skillful physician places a broken arm in a plaster cast to "manage" the mending process, so our failures must be given special attention until full restoration occurs. Any wrong move of the broken arm will create pain and lengthen the time of healing. Similarly, if we try to pull away from the tension God's discipline places on our broken areas, the pain will remind us of the need to stay in the harness of God.

Management is for the mature. Irresponsible people will not take the time, dedicate the energy, or redirect the funds necessary to manage their failures. Their usual policy is to blame others for their mistakes. But does it really matter who created the problem? By the time you've expended the energy to deduce who caused the mishap, the problem could have been compartmentalized, and management solutions could have been put in place. Your orientation must be solution-based, not blame-based. The Father's goal is that you learn your lesson. Taking the needed steps of correction will prove rewarding in many different ways. The primary benefit is that God becomes your Lord and you become His servant.

## PRINCIPLE #2: LET FAILURE HELP YOU BECOME A SERVANT OF GOD

Sherlock Holmes and Dr. Watson went on a camping trip. They arrived at their site and set up their tent. Later that night, Sherlock Holmes woke up Watson and said, "Watson, look up and tell me what you see."

Watson answered, "I see a dark sky full of stars."

Holmes asked him, "What does that tell you?"

Watson replied, "Well, sir, astronomically, it tells me that the universe is full of stars and planets. Astrologically, it tells me that Saturn is in Leo. Metaphysically, it tells me that the Lord is all-powerful to create such a vast universe and that we are an insignificant part of it. Meteorologically, it tells me that it is going to be clear and warm tomorrow."

Holmes was quiet for a moment, then said, "Watson, you idiot, somebody stole our tent."

At times, we act like Dr. Watson. We think we know it all. Yet our failures communicate loud and clear that we don't understand and we don't know it all. A know-it-all doesn't see the value in becoming a servant of God. Yet the know-it-all could avoid much heartache and pain by adopting this second principle of failure management.

The New Testament is replete with passages about the believer's role as a servant of Christ. In fact, the entire Bible is clear in its teachings on servanthood. But the fact of the matter is that no one wants to be a servant; all want to be served. We want to be served by God, by the church, by the gospel, and certainly by others. In fact, we use the Bible to support the faulty notion that we deserve to be served. Therefore, God's arduous task is to make servants out of His children. He's not so concerned about our completing various tasks of servitude, but rather that we develop the attitude of a servant.

The Bible gives us three distinctive traits of a servant. First, a servant is in a permanent relationship with his master. Second, a servant's will is swallowed up in the will of his master. Third, a servant lives to serve, even to the extent that he disregards his own interests.

## *Servanthood: A Permanent Relationship*

During the New Testament era, a sophisticated social structure existed for the maintenance of the slavery profession. The most familiar type of slave in this period was the *doulos*, or "bondslave." Paul referred to himself frequently as a servant (a *doulos*) of Jesus Christ because of his desire to give the Christians a practical illustration of how they ought to willingly put themselves in a position of servitude to Christ (Romans 1:1; Acts 26:16). True servants of Jesus Christ must pattern themselves after the model of submission which the *doulos* of that society portrayed openly before his master.

A Christian's ability to be successful in life is directly related to his or her obedience to God. Submission cannot be partial or inconsistent. In other words, you cannot say that you are walking in obedience to God simply because you obeyed Him once last year, or because you obey some of His commands. God wants to know that you are totally trustworthy and fully cooperative in every area. This is the reason that Paul referred to followers of Christ as "bondservants." A *doulos* was born into the condition of slavery. He knew no other life-style. His parents were slaves. Therefore, he was a slave. In Paul's day, the relationship of a master to a slave was permanent. The slave had to learn submission if he wanted to live. Compliance had to be forged into his character. And so it is with us. God wants to know that His orders will be carried out without adjustments or questions. He also wants to ensure that this kind of obedience is permanent, not merely an attempt to gain the perks one receives in serving God.

A story is told that there once was an opening with the CIA for an assassin. Such a highly classified position is difficult to fill, and there are many tests and background checks one must pass before he can even be considered. After sending just a few qualified applicants through the necessary training and testing, they narrowed the possible choices to two men and one woman—but only one position was available. The day came for the final test to determine which person would get the job.

The agent administering the test took one of the men to a large metal door and handed him a gun. "We must know that you'll follow our instructions, no matter what the circumstances," he explained. "Inside this room, you will find your wife sitting in a chair. Take this gun and kill her."

The man looked shocked and said, "You can't be serious! I could never shoot my own wife!"

"Well," said the CIA agent, "you're definitely not the right man for this job."

So they brought the second man in and handed him a gun. "We must know that you will follow instructions, no matter what the circumstances," they told him. "Inside you will find your wife sitting in a chair. Take this gun and kill her."

The second man looked a bit shocked, but nevertheless took the gun and went into the room. All was quiet for about five minutes; then the door opened. The man came out with tears in his eyes. "I tried, but I just couldn't pull the trigger on my own wife. I guess I'm not the right man for the job."

"No," the CIA agent replied. "You don't have what it takes. Take your wife and go home."

Now the only candidate left was the woman. So they led her to the same door and handed her the same gun. "We must be sure that you will follow instructions, no matter what the circumstances. This is your final test. Inside you will find your husband sitting in a chair. Take this gun and kill him."

The woman took the gun and opened the door. Before the door

was closed, the CIA agents heard the gun fire—one shot after another, thirteen shots in all. Then bedlam broke loose behind the door. They heard screaming, thrashing, banging on the walls. This went on for several minutes; then the room became eerily quiet. The door opened slowly, and there stood the woman. She wiped the sweat from her brow and said, "You guys didn't tell me the gun was loaded with blanks! I had to beat him to death with the chair!"

Quite obviously, God isn't calling us to be CIA agents or assassins. But He does want total allegiance to His orders on a permanent basis. A servant of God is a servant for life.

## Servanthood: The Submission of One's Will

A true bondservant is one who has identified with his master's will to such an extent that he does not have a will separate from that of his master. In other words, the servant's will has been completely submerged in knowing and doing the will of his master. To achieve this state of unity, a genuine, heartfelt yielding must take place in the volitional part of the servant's soul. Deep inside, the servant must acknowledge that his value and worth in life are gained by serving the will of his master.

The label "servant" may seem base and disrespectful, yet if you were the servant of a king, a powerful lord, or the president of a country, the position would be most enviable. The *doulos* gets worth and value from the One he serves—King Jesus. Thus, the title "servant of the Lord" is a powerful, well-respected one. Moses, Paul, and other biblical figures wore the title with pride and dignity. In fact, this designation became part of Paul's customary salutation when greeting the churches (Romans 1:1; Philippians 1:1). Paul embraced the reality of his being a servant of the Lord. His will was swallowed up in the will and service of his Master.

A young mother took her son shopping at the mall. As little boys often do, Johnny began running around the store, becoming disruptive to the other shoppers. Alice, his mother, got ahold of her son and said, "Johnny, sit down! Sit down!" Johnny just looked at her and continued doing what he was doing before.

In anger, Alice barked out a command: "Johnny, sit down immediately! Sit down, I said!" This time Johnny stopped running around and stood still where he was. As a final measure, Alice said, "If you don't sit down at once, when you get home I'm going to give you a spanking!" Reluctantly, Johnny sat down. But while seated in the chair, he looked up at his mother and said, "I'm sitting down on the outside, but I'm standing up on the inside!"

Johnny's response illustrates that there is a difference between submission and obedience. Johnny was obeying his mom's orders, but his heart was not in submission to her will. A true servant will synchronize his actions with his will and desires. His wishes will be in total submission to the will of his master.

## *Servanthood: Your Interests Are Your Master's Interests*

One day the manager of a large company noticed a new man on the job and asked him to come into his office. "What is your name?" the manager asked the new guy.

"Gary," the man replied.

The manager scowled. "Look, I don't know what kind of a place you worked for before, but I don't call anyone by his first name. It breeds familiarity, and that leads to a breakdown in authority. I refer to my employees by their last names only—Smith, Jones, Baker. That's all. I'm to be referred to as Mr. Robertson. Now that we've got that straight, what is your last name?"

The new guy smirked. "Darling. My name is Gary Darling."

"Okay—er, Gary, the next thing I want to tell you is—"

Gary may have wanted to comply with the desires of his boss, but he showed his boss that it wasn't going to work—not with a last name like "Darling"! In your case, however, whatever God desires concerning your life will work all the time—for you and for Him.

A *doulos* has one interest in life—his master's. How would you feel being a permanent servant without a will of your own? I'm sure the feeling wouldn't be a pleasant one. Yet the bondservant works with an attitude of joy and delight. Nothing excites him as much as his master's business.

The word *interest* conveys the idea of a pursuit, a mission, an objective, goal, or dream. The bondservant identifies so strongly with his master's interests that he freely dies to his own and takes possession of his master's. Because of this, the master can trust the servant to handle delicate matters, make significant decisions, or even run his entire business or household. The servant, in essence, has become like a trusted partner; he has the master's heart.

What opportunities are you missing because you haven't died to your own interests? Throughout any time of failure, there are key opportunities God makes available according to your degree of obedience to Him. The Lord is looking for people He can trust with great tasks and blessings. The prerequisite, however, is that you pass the test of obeying God's leadership, even in times of failure. It's easy to listen to God when all is going well. How about when nothing is going your way? Does your pride force you to take full command of your life? Or can you believe that this all-knowing, omnipotent God is capable of guiding your life through the valley of the shadow of death and into green pastures? Trust must be established in times of chaos. True intimacy with the Lord is forged when you let go of your security blanket and hold on to the hem of His garment.

# ── Chapter 5 ──

# BRINGING ORDER
# OUT OF CHAOS

*The ability to get into trouble and the ability to get out of
trouble are seldom present in the same person.*

*—Author Unknown*

**M**arty was so exhausted after work that all he could think
about was getting home, taking a hot shower, and eating
his dinner. But right after his meal, his six-year-old son
started to tug on his arm. "Come on, Dad, let's play," said little Steven.
"No, Son, not now. Perhaps later," came the reply. Steven pouted as he
walked away.

In another five minutes, Steven returned to ask his dad to play.
"Okay, Dad, it's later now. Let's play."

"Not now, Son. Dad's tired! Maybe later," shouted Marty. Steven
frowned as he went off to his room to play by himself.

Five minutes later, Steven returned again to ask his dad to play.
Before his son could say a word, Marty spotted the Sunday paper on
the coffee table. There was a map of the world on the top page. "Steven,
I know how you like jigsaw puzzles," said Marty. At that, he tore the
picture of the world map into many pieces and told his son to go to his
bedroom and complete the puzzle. "After you've put the map of the
world together, I'll play with you," said Marty.

Smiling to himself, Marty turned his attention to the evening news. But to his surprise, Steven returned to the family room in a few minutes with the puzzle completed. Marty asked, "Son, how were you able to finish the puzzle so quickly?"

Steven replied, "Well, Dad, on the other side of the map of the world was a picture of a man. When I put the man together, the whole world came together."

Just as this young boy quickly made sense out of what appeared to be a mess, God takes the fragments of our failure and uses them to bring us a step closer to our destiny. Time is the best tool in His toolbox to help us sort through chaos. Time has a way of proving all things. A premature evaluation of your failure can cause you to draw the wrong conclusion about the direction your life should take. A delay does not mean a denial. If this simple reality is true, now is the time to formulate a strategy to bring order out of the chaos your failure has created.

Man has been given an innate creative ability to make sense out of disorder. The first man, Adam, was given the responsibility of naming all the animals. Imagine coming up with a new name for every beast and bird created by God! Prior to the Fall, man enjoyed a high level of artistic freedom. Although sin affected every aspect of human behavior after the Fall, creativity still flourished—albeit at a lower level. The introduction of sin, along with its consequences, always dulls one's senses and lessens one's ability to function at peak performance. The heart becomes darkened because of the breach in relationship with God and His many blessings (Psalm 51:11–12). Through Adam, God shows us that He encourages the development of our creativity as well. The punishment that subsequently was given to Adam required human creativity (Genesis 3:17–21). In order to farm the land for food, as Adam was instructed, one must have both wisdom and survival skills.

### COMPARTMENTALIZE YOUR PROBLEM

A middle-aged woman was sitting in her den when a small black snake slithered across the floor and under the couch. The woman was deathly afraid of snakes, so she ran to the bathroom to get her husband, who was taking a shower.

The man of the house came running from the shower to the den, with only a towel around his waist. Taking an old broom handle, he began poking under the couch to retrieve the snake. At this point the family dog, which had been sleeping, awoke and became excited. In the dog's frenzy over the actions of the husband, the little terrier touched his cold nose to the back of the man's heel. Surmising that the snake had outmaneuvered him and bitten him on the heel, the man fainted dead away.

The wife concluded that her husband had had a heart attack because of his physical exertion in trying to kill the snake. She ran from the house to the hospital emergency room, which was only a block away. The paramedics soon arrived at the house and placed the man, now semiconscious, on a stretcher.

As the paramedics carried the man out of the den, the snake reappeared from beneath the couch. At this point, one of the medics became so excited that he dropped his end of the stretcher and broke the leg of the husband.[1]

As zany as that story is, imagine how it might have ended had any of the characters compartmentalized the situation. Any problem can be handled when it's contained and restricted from bleeding into the other areas of life. Most people, however, panic during a crisis. When this occurs, they tend to view every aspect of their lives through the disorder created by the initial problem. Disorder can be compartmentalized by determining the cause of the problem. Once the cause of your failure has been determined, you should take the necessary measures to restrict its negative effects on the other areas of your life.

If, for example, you're dealing with a child who is using drugs, this doesn't mean that your whole family is falling apart. Neither does it mean that you are a bad parent. It simply means that one child is having a problem. Limit the proliferation of the problem by talking frankly with the child and by taking steps to decrease the impact of this problem on the rest of the family. Also talk to the other family members who may be aware of or affected by the drug use of the one child. The family will survive and experience victory. But to ensure victory in this matter or in any crisis situation, quick action must be taken.

Don't procrastinate or minimize the situation. Crisis calls for action. Wise strategic and tactical action can even save lives. If it means that the child has to go to a drug rehabilitation clinic, take him! If it means that you have to join a support group, join one! Whatever solution the problem calls for, don't waver. Move on it as soon as possible. The sooner the firefighters respond to an alarm, the sooner the fire is brought under control. A controlled crisis is a solvable crisis. The faster you move to bring your crisis under control, the faster your life gets back to normal.

In order to stabilize your crisis, you must understand your dilemma. Oftentimes people react without really understanding their problems. People tend to have knee-jerk reactions rather than seeking true solutions. Sometimes you just have to put out the fires in your life. And in times like these, whatever you can get your hands on is what you're going to toss on the flames. But in most cases, crises don't just sneak up on people. The Hollywood perspective of life isn't real life. It's contrived. Real life has lots of down time. In real life, the bad guys aren't always chasing you at breakneck speed. There's time to set up a plan of attack or a solution for any dilemma that comes your way.

## FIND SOMETHING TO CELEBRATE

Several years ago, I counseled a young married couple going through a tough time in their relationship. Throughout the session, they went back and forth taking subtle jabs at one another. Finally I stopped them and said, "Let's move toward a solution." They both agreed. I then asked the wife to look at her husband and find something nice to say about him. She stared at him for a moment and said, "I like your glasses." I couldn't help but chuckle. My intention was for her to see some hope in the relationship, and a nice pair of eyeglasses doesn't bring hope! But in their case, I said, "I'll take it. It's a starting point." Tough situations call for creative thinking.

How do you see the things around you? Do you look at your life through a lens of pleasure or pain? Can you find something good in the midst of chaos? Or is everything horrible? The apostle Paul instructs us to adopt a positive perspective on life with this advice: "Finally, brothers, whatever is true, whatever is noble, whatever is right, whatever is pure, whatever is lovely, whatever is admirable—if anything is excellent or praiseworthy—think about such things" (Philippians 4:8). This concept of life makes us look for the flowers on the rose bush, not the thorns. We are pressed to find something in our chaos that we can still celebrate. And there is always something that can provoke us to praise.

## RESTORING THE CATHEDRAL

In 1994 our church purchased a historic Romanesque cathedral from a Baptist congregation. Our congregation was eight years old at the time of the purchase, and we had been meeting in a catering hall. We needed a building that could seat approximately a thousand people, although our church numbered about five hundred people at the time. Because of our location in northern New Jersey, just thirty minutes west of New York City, real estate comes at a premium. So we rejoiced at finding this old cathedral.

The congregation that previously owned the building had dwindled to approximately forty or fifty people. They did not have the resources to properly care for this former architectural showpiece. The cathedral had become infested with bats and rodents. The roof had many leaks, and the stenciled ceilings were chipped and discolored. The hand-painted murals depicting celestial scenes were peeling off the walls and ceilings. Looking at the building in its neglected state would cause any artist or lover of great architecture to weep.

After the closing, we found that there were more problems with this building than we had anticipated. Old plaster walls have a great way of hiding electrical and environmental problems buried within. For the first two years of our occupancy, we were only able to make the monthly mortgage payments, pay our overhead, and pocket a one-cent surplus. The leaky roof, frequent electrical failures, lack of carpeting, and many other things annoyed me daily. No substantial repairs took place during that time.

Preaching in the sanctuary was an acoustical nightmare. Because we didn't have the funds to install an appropriate sound system, half the congregation would hear what I said a few seconds after the other half. There was actually a time delay in the room. If I told a joke, half the people would laugh immediately, and the other half missed it because they couldn't hear what I said. Even when a few seconds passed, the joke was no longer intelligible because the sound was muddied by the laughter of the people up front. Those who couldn't hear were upset. It was as if someone was robbing them of a good time. So they began to laugh based on the cues provided by those who had heard the joke!

I'm the type of person who must have things done in an orderly manner. My mind is very tidy. During this confusing period of time, I had to find something to celebrate so that my crisis would not consume me. Several things came to mind. I began to take a greater interest in mentoring and training people. If the money wasn't there to restore and renovate the building, why not spend the time building people and developing leaders? Rather than becoming depressed and overwhelmed, I saw the church grow in strength and intimacy. The parishioners focused on the essentials of serving people rather than on the need to beautify the building. The trap of becoming engulfed by the chaos was avoided through celebration. It was a joy getting to know people and their leadership potential. But first I had to get my mind and sights off my trial and on something pleasurable.

What are the joyous things you're overlooking because of the demands of your trial? Your trial or failure should not control you. Rather, you should be the one dictating your actions, responses, and how you will spend your time and energy. Look around. Perhaps during this crisis you can spend some extra time with your grandchildren or get back to taking those music lessons you used to enjoy so much. Schedule time for the fun things in life.

You must take control of your schedule. During a crisis, depressing thoughts and behaviors have a way of monopolizing our time. Break out of the cycle of gloom. Do something adventurous and fun. Don't procrastinate about having fun. Just do it! Your crisis doesn't own you. It cannot rule the way you respond. It's your choice to celebrate or sulk. What's it going to be, a cell or a celebration? Life can either be a prison or a place of praise. Choose! Make a decision! Live your life! Enjoy yourself! I did! And I received victory over my circumstances.

After two very lean years, our congregation was able to raise the necessary funds to renovate and restore the building to beyond its former glory. Now when I take someone on a tour of the cathedral, it appears impressive and stately. They see the glory, but they don't know the real story!

## GOD IS BIGGER THAN YOUR CRISIS

When we think about the great minds in history—the likes of Einstein, Edison, and Aristotle— most can agree, with wide-eyed amazement, that God is the creator of geniuses. There are no words to adequately describe the ingenuity of God. Perhaps this is the reason He declared, "As the heavens are higher than the earth, so are my *ways* higher than your ways and my *thoughts* than your thoughts" (Isaiah 55:9, emphasis added). The Hebrew word for *ways* can refer to roads, courses of life, modes of action, and manners. The word *higher* means "to soar, to be lofty, to mount up, and to rise up to great height." The Hebrew word for *thoughts* connotes an ingenious plan, an imagination, a plot, a curious work, or an intention. When these meanings are joined, they shed greater understanding on the two points Isaiah was making in verse nine.

First, God's course of life soars above ours. His mode of action mounts up above that of a mere mortal. How God behaves and lives is beyond our finite comprehension. What God does and how He acts are incomprehensible from a human perspective. We cannot understand His behavior. It soars too high above ours. Second, His ingenious plans and imaginations are raised to heights greatly above ours. God's thoughts are curious works to us. They reflect intentions that are above our mental capabilities. We simply cannot think on His level, no matter how smart we may appear to be. The thoughts that God thinks would never enter our minds, even in seed form. Since our ways are not God's ways and our thoughts are not His thoughts, we should simply take a permanent posture of faith, rather than one of unbelief or fear. Failure has a way of creating in our minds a sense of chaos and disorder. Comfort is found in the fact that God takes pleasure in fixing things that we cannot begin to sort out.

## EVERY CRISIS IS CONTROLLED

The Bible is emphatic on this point: God is at work in your times of chaos, whether you're cognizant of it or not. This is because God has placed boundaries around every crisis. He has determined the length and severity of every problem. Things that you anticipated and planned to accomplish may have blown up in your face. Your life may have surprised you by taking an unexpected 180-degree turn. When failure strikes, all you see are hopelessness and ruin. Yet when things calm down, you'll begin to see that your crisis is really controlled. It cannot go beyond a certain point.

God is so good at solving problems that it can seem as if He thrives in an environment of disorder. In our pain, we become more sensitive to His abilities and power. In our pain, we cry out to Him more honestly, hoping for some kind of favorable response. C. S. Lewis addressed how God reacts to human pain, writing, "God whispers to us in our pleasure, speaks to us in our consciousness, and shouts to us in our pain." It is in our pain that we draw near to Him, looking for comfort, answers, and hope. His voice sounds clearer because of our desperate situation.

When we comprehend the genius of God, we cannot hold to the painful position of doubt and fear. There is no inherent benefit in doubting. Dale Carnegie once told of interviewing Henry Ford when Ford was seventy-eight years of age. He had expected to find a gaunt, nervous old man. When asked if he worried, Ford replied, "No. I believe God is managing affairs and He doesn't need any advice from me.

87

With God in charge, I believe that everything will work out for the best in the end. So what is there to worry about?"[2]

Ford's observation drives home the point: Every crisis is controlled. There are limits to each problem's devastation and ruin. Keep your cool; God is still in control. Your knowledge of His ways will help you to cope and stay calm during times of chaos.

## EVERY CRISIS IS SCHEDULED

God is an artist who seeks to gain glory out of repairing and beautifying our lives. No matter how great the confusion, He is not afraid to get involved. Artists create. They invent. Mankind is God's greatest creation! God is not to be rushed when He's creating a masterpiece that is unique from all of His other works of grace. God sees us as collector's items, individually numbered. Each person's destiny is distinctly different from anyone else's. Yet God the Artist knows what each person needs for a rich and satisfying life.

God knows when trials are coming and when they are ending. There's a schedule to the execution of His master plan of our lives. And although we don't know the times and seasons of our testing, we do know that God has a master plan for us.

Like most creators, God is inventive. He can create masterpieces out of slim-to-none resources. Your ignorance of a divine schedule does not negate God's readiness to help you through a chaotic period. Every emergency is under His control. God doesn't have panic attacks. He's always calm and cool—ready for anything and everything. He is keeping track of everything and is always resourceful. No matter what the problem calls for, He's prepared. Dedicate yourself to His leadership, and don't compromise the wisdom He uses to guide you through life's awkward moments. Although we're often blind to His direction and schedule, God sees and understands our needs.

Genesis introduces God by describing the fact that it was He who created the heavens and the earth in the beginning (Genesis 1:1). In the Bible account of creation, two alternating Hebrew words, *bara* and *asah,* were used to describe how God created the world. Hebrew scholar War-ren Baker writes, "*Bara* conveys the thought of creation *ex nihilio* (out of nothing), while *asah* is broader in scope and deals with refinement. In other words, the emphasis was on fashioning the created objects."[3]

In Genesis 1:1, the word *create* is *bara.* This means that God created the heavens and the earth out of nothing. No existent matter was used to produce the physical earth or heaven. This phenomenal aspect of God's nature tells us that our failures are never beyond God's resourcefulness. If necessary, He will simply create solutions out of nothing in order to meet our needs and keep His schedule.

On the other hand, God can also *create (asah)* refinement out of the chaos precipitated by our failures. In Genesis 1:7, God used the word *made (asah)* to describe how He created the sky by separating out the water. The creative eyes of God saw a body of water and conceived that by refining its structure, mass, and placement, the sky could be formed. With such a wonderfully creative God, you have no need to fear in any situation or circumstance. He is capable of handling anything that comes your way, because every crisis takes place under His watch-ful eye. And every crisis is scheduled; nothing catches Him off guard.

## EVERY CRISIS HAS A PURPOSE

The will of God is very personal, to such an extent that often only the recipient can discern its proper fit. God leads each of His children down an individualized path. No two people will automatically get the same response from God, even if their situations are identical. No two situations befalling the same person will call for the same solution. God has a specific plan for each of us, and He leads us in such unique ways that we have to constantly pray for guidance and reassurance.

Crises serve God's purposes for our lives. Since He holds the master plan for our lives, nothing can interfere with our purpose unless it is in sync with our destiny. No, God doesn't create every crisis or disruption that comes our way. But He does safeguard His divine purposes for our lives. Trials are His servants. They serve His will and are at His direction. Nothing can thwart His plan or alter His desires. God is supreme, and His divine purpose for each of us is being served through our times of failure. Our role is to trust Him and try to determine His purpose in allowing the crisis. Only you can fully understand God's purpose for your life and His intention with your crisis.

About two years after I came to faith in Christ, I began having unusual feelings about studying for the ministry. I say that these feelings were unusual because I was then a graduate student pursuing a master's degree in civil engineering. I was not planning to change my major to religion or transfer to a seminary. I was just trying to sort out the strong attraction I was having for preaching and the ministry.

At the time, a math professor was in charge of the Christian group on campus. I asked him what he thought of my going into the ministry. "There are too many ministers already," he said. "We don't need another church or pastor. We just need for the existing churches to fulfill their purpose." At that, I became more confused. How could I abandon the idea of the ministry when my feelings were so strong and unrelenting? Since he was a highly respected Christian authority on our campus, I prayed about what he said. As a young Christian, I didn't know how to respond to his counsel. I was also quite intimidated because he was so knowledgeable of the Bible and strong in his faith in God. Yet the feelings I was having did not leave, even though I now wanted them to.

Someone once asked me, "What does the voice of God sound like?" I told him, "It's the voice that keeps bothering you." God kept bothering me about the ministry. After graduation, I decided to pursue the thoughts I was having. While continuing in my engineering career, I began studying and serving in the local church, pursuing the gnawing feeling that I eventually realized was the will of God for my life. I learned a valuable lesson. No one can truly know the will of God for your life but you. In my crisis of confusion, the purpose of God for my life became clear. Without this time of internal uncertainty and up-heaval, I would not have known my calling. This book would not have been written had I not learned firsthand that every crisis has a purpose.

God offers us free assistance—especially during a crisis. Yet many people unconsciously refuse His input and care. They are blinded to the assistance available until the pressure of the crisis opens their eyes to the reality of God's love. God's care is intended to provide us with answers during our moments of chaos. His care also establishes changes in our outlook, character, and expectations—making them far healthier than before the disorder was created. Our goal should not only be to create order out of our chaos, but also to learn the invaluable lessons that can only be taught during times of disruption.

## EVERY CRISIS BRINGS VALUABLE LESSONS

One lesson we learn in a crisis is humility. Humility is an ac-knowledgment of God's involvement and an acceptance of His divine intentions. Humility is directing praise toward God rather than toward oneself. In contrast, pride is what comes across when we take center stage during the victories or failures we experience.

During a very confusing time in his life, the prophet Elijah had to run and take cover in a cave. Wicked Queen Jezebel had put a hit out on him. The day prior to the issuing of this death threat, God had used Elijah to work a great miracle in Israel. This feat led thousands of people back to an intimate relationship with God (1 Kings 18–19). The queen was angry at the display of God's power and the death of her paid psychics and false prophets. In Elijah's flight, humility was being formed in his character.

God had not forewarned this great prophet about Jezebel's response to his victory, nor was he told where to run after the murderous threat was issued. Elijah just ran to the wilderness, hoping to find a place of safety and rejuvenation. Perplexed about God's ways, Elijah became extremely discouraged. Perhaps this is why he prayed, *"I have had enough, LORD...Take my life; I am no better than my ancestors"* (1 Kings 19:4). F. W. Krummacher, in his classic work on Elijah, wrote, "Thick darkness hung over the prophet's soul. This is shown by his whole conduct—a close reserve, his desire for solitude, his planless wandering into the gloomy wilderness, all indicate a discouraged and dejected state of mind. Perplexed with regard to his vocation—even with respect to God and his government—his soul lies in the midst of a thousand doubts and distressing thoughts."[4]

Quite discouraged, the prophet was wondering how his ministry in Israel could remain effective now that he was running for his life. Elijah didn't know that God was working humility into his character. All he felt was that he'd been made a national spectacle. Keep in mind that God's ways are higher than your ways. Even in your discouragement and confusion, God is still at work developing a masterpiece. Humility is a beautiful garment. When worn, it produces a great fruitfulness that ensures your continued success.

Oftentimes, your trials and failures may make you appear foolish, impractical, or weak. Failure has a way of forcing you to reevaluate your actions and behavior. It gets you in touch with your deepest

values and brings you face-to-face with the cornerstone of your existence. Making this adjustment, however, puts you in a very precarious
situation. You don't have answers for your crisis. "I'm trusting God" is
the only sentence you can muster in response to the flurry of questions
posed by the people around you. In such times of emotional chaos, you
may even need to convince yourself that there is hope. "I believe that
God cares for me and wants to help me through this chaos" is a good
thought that will carry you through some of the negativity you may
encounter during this humility-building stage. Saying it will release
faith and hope into your heart. Making this statement will help you see
that humility has already begun its penetrating work in your life. You
are now acknowledging your need for and dependence on God. That's
progress! You're growing spiritually!

Also, keep in mind that God sees the big picture. You and I only
see the present reality. Humility is an attitude of trust on your part
toward God. Pride is the temptation to manipulate your way out of the
uncanny and embarrassing circumstance, in order to save face. To in-
form people that you're trusting God may sound foolish. To add insult
to injury, you may feel a bit silly because you have no knowledge of
when your situation will improve or change. Yet you hear and obey the
call to walk in humility. Congratulations! You're looking beyond the
present distress and seeing a higher plan. Your character is being honed
and developed. This is one of the ways in which order is created out of
chaos. Your life is becoming prioritized by values, rather than materialistic achievements.

## EVERY CRISIS BRINGS SOMETHING SPECIAL FROM GOD

The adult children of a prominent family decided to give their
father a book of the family's history as a birthday present. They com-

missioned a professional biographer to do the work, carefully warning him of the family's one "black sheep"—Uncle George, who had been executed in the electric chair for murder.

The biographer assured the children, "I can handle that situation so that there will be no embarrassment. I'll merely say that Uncle George occupied a chair of applied electronics at an important government institution. He was attached to his position by the strongest of ties and his death came as a real shock!"[5]

Have you ever thought that there are some things in your life that are best left untold? Well, throughout the Bible noble men and women—namely, David, Paul, Peter, and Sarah—experienced lessons in humility through painful and awkward dilemmas. Each of their situations was initially embarrassing. But following their failures, they understood that God had been directing their anxious steps all along. Don't apologize for past or present circumstances in your life—even if they make you uncomfortable. God will use them for a greater purpose—for something special in the future. Just wait and see.

During a dark period in David's life when he did not understand the chaos engulfing him, he fled Israel and went to Achish, the king of Gath, seeking political asylum. Rather than granting David's request for protection, the heathen king wanted to make his head a trophy on the wall. At this period in history, David was a mighty, world-acclaimed warrior in the army of Israel. To avoid being murdered, he had to pretend he was insane. The Bible says, *"While he was in their hands he acted like a madman, making marks on the doors of the gate and letting saliva run down his beard"* (1 Samuel 21:13). Imagine the mighty David allowing saliva to run down his beard in public! Here was the military hero—the subject of numerous victory songs and dances—behaving like a fool in order to spare his life. Humbling? You'd better believe it! David did whatever it took in order to preserve his life and destiny.

His actions, although humiliating, were intended to spare his life. Was God caring for David during this crisis? Yes! However, an unspiritual outsider observing David's antics might not have thought so. This skeptic likely would have asked another question: "What kind of a caring God would allow this embarrassment to happen to one of His sons?" A person who understands God's nature would reply, "God's ways are higher than your ways. Before you judge God, wait until the end of David's trial. At that time, ask your questions."

Like David, I'd prefer to play the role of a fool temporarily while God works something special in my life, rather than keep up my act as a boastful loser. After his period of confusion, David took his place on the throne as king of Israel. The throne was the special thing God had in mind for David all along. Throughout the trial, God was working the principle of submission into David's life. God's plans for us, too, seem nonsensical at times. Yet the outcome always justifies the means. Submission to God's oversight and leadership is a priceless lesson.

Your trial may cause some temporary humiliation because it takes some seemingly foolish acts to overcome failure—like joining a support group or apologizing to an angry son for not being there for him—but hang in there. God has something special in mind for you. His care will be evident in the character development lessons you'll learn during this chaotic time of your life.

# Chapter 6

# WHO CAN YOU TURN TO ?

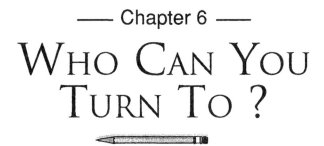

*Lots of people want to ride with you in the limo,*
*but what you want is someone who will take the*
*bus with you when the limo breaks down.*

*—Oprah Winfrey*

T he role of an encourager is one of the most vital roles in life. Without encouragers, leaders would not be able to function, society would not develop, and our world would not advance. Encouragers, whether great or small, blow wind into the sails of other people. Through their powerful words, hope is established in the hearts of the discouraged. Their comforting words enable the recipients to overcome hurdles and avoid detours. Although encouragers don't have the answers to all of life's difficulties, they feed the troubled person with nourishing doses of "chicken soup for the soul." Their words of solace fuel the discouraged person, enabling him to conquer trials, overcome adversity, and win untold battles against failure. Yet the significant contributions of these unique people often go uncelebrated.

Encouraging words are like money invested in the stock market. The investment communicates what you believe. If you believe that a particular stock has no future, you won't purchase shares in it. But if you think a stock has a bright future, you'll scrape up money from every conceivable source to register your opinion.

I always tell my daughters that they are leaders. They have been hearing this message since birth. When my daughter Danielle was about ten years old, I asked her to clean off the coffee table in the family room. To my surprise, upon my return, the entire room was cleaned. I said, "Danielle, you're a leader! You didn't only do what I asked, you did what was needed." She walked out of that room feeling ten feet tall. My words, a natural response to her hard work, had encouraged her.

Encouragement cannot be a canned response. No one will be encouraged by rehearsed statements. The recipient will feel that the sentiments are insincere, and he'll probably be right! One day when I was working as a civil engineer, I came back from lunch to find a hastily scribbled note on my desk. My boss had just read a report I had worked on and dropped me a line conveying his thoughts. Although this occurred some ten years ago, I'm still encouraged by the memory of that note today. It was spontaneous, heartfelt, and to the point. Though he never knew how his note encouraged me, it fueled me for weeks to come.

Henry Ford once said that the ability to encourage others is one of life's finest assets. The inventor and manufacturer of the automobile knew the power of encouragement. He had learned it as a young man. He remembered well the time at the beginning of his career, when he made a drawing of his newly built engine for Thomas Edison. Young Ford had endured criticism and ridicule. Most mechanical experts of that day were convinced that electric carriages would be the popular passenger cars of the future. But at a dinner one evening when Edison was present, Ford began explaining his engine to the men nearest him at the table. He noticed that Edison, seated several chairs away, was listening. Finally the great man moved closer and asked the young inventor to make a drawing. When the crude sketch was complete, Edison studied it intently, then suddenly banged his fist on the table. "Young man," he said, "that's the thing! You have it!" Ford recalled years later, "The thump of that fist upon the table was worth worlds to me."[1]

When Sir Walter Scott was a boy, he was considered a great dullard. His accustomed place in the schoolroom was the ignominious dunce corner, where a tall, pointed cap adorned his head. When Scott was twelve or thirteen years old, he happened to be in a house where some famous literary guests were being entertained. Robert Burns, the Scottish poet, was admiring a picture under which was written the couplet of a stanza. He inquired about the identity of the author. No one seemed to know. Timidly, a boy crept up to his side, named the author, and quoted the rest of the poem. Burns was surprised and delighted. Laying his hand on the boy's head, he exclaimed, "Ah, brainie, ye will be a great man in Scotland some day." From that day on, Walter Scott was a changed lad. One word of encouragement had set him on the road to greatness.[2]

A talented, red-haired Polish lad wanted to be a pianist. However, his teachers at the conservatory gave him no encouragement. He was told that his fingers were too short and thick for the piano. Later he bought a cornet. The same criticism was given to him, along with the suggestion that he try another instrument. Passed around like a hot potato, he went back to the piano. Embittered and discouraged, he happened to meet the famous composer and pianist Anton Rubinstein. The young Pole played for him. Rubinstein praised and encouraged him. The lad promised to practice seven hours a day. Rubinstein's words of praise changed the entire world of Jan Paderewski.[3]

While these success stories serve to support my assertions on the power of encouragement, they can also convey the opposite of what I intend. Some reader—caught in the viselike grip of failure—may wait around for his big break, hoping someone famous will spot him in the crowd and call him forth. The odds of that happening, however, are extremely slim. Success is not achieved because someone successful notices you and offers a few sentences of advice. Success is achieved when you find fulfillment in the very thing you were created to do.

I remember the story of a multimillionaire who was being interviewed on the topic "How to make the American dream work for you." He said, "When my wife and I got married, we only had five cents to our name. I left my apartment one afternoon with the hopes of finding something that could make me successful. I came across a guy selling apples. So I bought an apple with the only five cents I had. I took it home and polished it for several hours until it became extremely shiny. I was able to sell it for ten cents. With the ten cents I went out and bought two apples. I took those two apples to my apartment and cleaned and shined them."

The interviewer jumped in and asked, "So, is that how you got rich?"

"No," said the multimillionaire, "my wealthy father-in-law died and left me several million dollars."

Don't be moved by the appearance of success until you learn the real story. All of us want to be encouraged. But don't look in the places that have a pie-in-the-sky view of encouragement. You may never find it there.

## HOW TO RECOGNIZE ENCOURAGERS

Hebrews cautions us with these words: *"Do not forget to entertain strangers, for by so doing some people have entertained angels without knowing it"* (Hebrews 13:2). Encouragers don't wear signs that say "encourager." They are ordinary people just like you and me. In fact, each of us can cite a time when someone we barely knew gave us kind words of encouragement. For this reason, Hebrews forewarns us about our attitudes when interacting with strangers and casual acquaintances. The point of this verse is that something powerful can transpire in an atmosphere of casualness. If you aren't careful, you can easily overlook the significance of a stranger's words.

Some of us tend to place more value on encouragement from high profile individuals. Rarely will we accept an encouraging word spoken by an acquaintance or a subordinate. The majority of people will not even consider these individuals as sources of hope. Consequently, the affirmation needed to overcome a trying situation will go unnoticed because of the messenger's social status. The real issue, however, is not the messenger's level of importance, but the recipient's perspective on encouragement. True encouragement is not when a high profile person lends a helping hand to someone a few rungs down on the ladder of success. Rather, it comes whenever genuine care and concern are expressed by one human being for another.

Early on in the life of the church that I pastor, my small congregation needed a place to hold its Sunday and midweek services. So I took out the yellow pages and let my fingers do the walking. I began calling churches with the hope that someone would allow us to rent worship space every Sunday afternoon. While I was busy making these telephone calls, my mind was also debating the possibility of my going back to school. After completing a master's degree in engineering several years prior, I had vowed that I would never go back to school again. I was tired of the intensity of academic training. Although I had made that vow to myself, God had been dealing with me for weeks about going to seminary. I was doing my best to ignore Him.

After my fifth or sixth inquiry, I contacted a minister who was quite apologetic that he didn't have any space to rent our fledgling group. Before he hung up, he asked if I had been to seminary. Upon hearing my negative reply, he spent the next ten minutes encouraging me to go to seminary. He listed a number of benefits of a good seminary education, one of which was that it would help our church immensely.

When the conversation ended, I walked away thoroughly encouraged about attending seminary. At that point, I forgot about making calls for worship space because my mind was preoccupied with what the pastor had said. I came out of the den and announced to my wife that I would be going to seminary. She had a tough time making the connection between inquiries about rental space and my immediate decision to go back to school. Although I didn't know the pastor who had given me the advice and have never heard from him again, one thing I do know is that his words of encouragement resulted in my attending and completing seminary. I'm glad I didn't forget to entertain strangers.

Wasn't it Balaam's donkey (Numbers 22:28) that spoke supernatural words of warning, saving the life of a money-hungry prophet? If God can use a donkey, he certainly can use intelligent human beings to affirm you during a period of discouragement. It simply requires that you be open to other people, despite how you are feeling about yourself.

Ordinary people are as qualified as extraordinary people in speaking a needed word. Perhaps you have been ignoring the encouragement coming from your gasoline station attendant, newspaper deliverer, coworker, younger brother, or student. Each of these individuals can be a source of motivation. Don't overlook them because of familiarity or the subordinate roles they play in your life. Such an attitude is not in concert with the kingdom of God. The kingdom comprises all kinds of ordinary people known as servants of God. Each provides a significant contribution to the quality of life in the kingdom.

## WHAT DOES ENCOURAGEMENT ACCOMPLISH?

### *Encouragement Is a Facilitator of Hope*

Encouragement is not simply optimism; it's much more than that. An optimist thinks positively about everything and everyone despite the circumstances. Optimism is passive. If you're not careful, it can make you avoid problems in the hope that they will clear up on their own. The optimist quietly believes in a better outcome or improved situation.

Encouragement, on the other hand, is a facilitator of hope. It lifts you up by causing you to think on a higher plane. Encouragement helps you to gather your internal fortitude and the resources lying dormant within, so that your goals can be realized and achieved. Encouragement moves you to action and faith. It reshapes your thinking—from hopelessness and despair to the possibilities before you. Norman Vincent Peale said, "Become a 'possibilitarian.' No matter how dark things seem to be or actually are, raise your sights and see the possibilities—always see them, for they are always there."[4]

Receiving encouragement is like seeing land after months at sea. Encouragement communicates hope. While it may not provide a solution to your dilemma, it gives you a newfound momentum as you continue on your journey. Many people give up when the fuel of hope has been depleted. Encouragers are like fueling stations along the way to one's destiny. God has them stationed intermittently throughout your life, just so that you can receive enough strength to go on. The key is to recognize and accept their words of solace.

The apostle Paul was a superb encourager. One person he regularly refueled was his spiritual son Timothy. Paul's second letter to Timothy was written from a Roman prison. Imagine a man in prison encouraging someone in the outside world! Paul didn't let his incarceration limit his ability to encourage someone else. When your purpose is clear and your perspective of the situation is godly, nothing can discourage you—not even limited mobility.

Paul wrote to Timothy, *"I thank God, whom I serve, as my forefathers did, with a clear conscience, as night and day I constantly remember you in my prayers. Recalling your tears, I long to see you, so that I may be filled with joy"* (2 Timothy 1:3–4). With these heartfelt words from the salutation alone, Timothy was affirmed. Imagine the aged apostle taking a personal interest in a young man and praying for him both night and day. If I'd been in Timothy's shoes, I would have been extremely encouraged just in the fact that Paul was thinking of me—let alone praying for me! His prayers would be like icing on the cake.

Further analysis of Paul's prayers would lead us to conclude that Timothy was someone with a bright future. Prayer is the voicing of one's hope to the Lord. It communicates the desire for the impossible to become possible. Paul was conveying his desire for the Lord to move in Timothy's life in a most powerful way. Paul's state of imprisonment did not degrade him in Timothy's eyes. Rather, it elevated him. This encouragement surely proved to increase Timothy's hope.

## Encouragement Affirms the Person

Encouragers affirm other people. Their soothing words challenge the recipient to look for options and possibilities rather than giving up. True encouragement is communicating, in some fashion, the statement "I believe in you." Discouragement, on the other hand, is the absence of affirmation. The word *discouragement* comes from the prefix *dis,* which means "to fail or to cease," and the word *courage,* which means "the attitude of facing and dealing with anything recognized as dangerous, difficult, or painful." Discouragement, then, is failing to face something difficult or painful. Consequently, when true words of encouragement are spoken, they give the hearer the strength needed to face the circumstances.

Using Paul's second letter to Timothy as a model of encouragement, we can see how the apostle incorporated affirming thoughts in his introductory remarks. He wrote, *"I have been reminded of your sincere faith, which first lived in your grandmother Lois and in your mother Eunice and, I am persuaded, now lives in you also"* (2 Timothy 1:5). In other words, Paul was saying to Timothy, "I know you. You're not hypocritical. You're real, and your faith is genuine."

Paul's affirmation of Timothy's sincere faith was another way of saying, "I know that you'll handle things justly, no matter what comes your way." Paul's casual remarks to Timothy affirmed his faith, affirmed him as a person of unquestionable devotion to the things of God. Paul believed in Timothy. This kind of affirmation is crucial to overcoming the negative thoughts that usually surface in times of failure. An inevitable by-product of failure is the erosion of self-esteem. Questions begin to eat at your self-worth. They challenge your sense of competency, intelligence, and insight. When the self-esteem is damaged, depression is sure to follow. Depression makes you feel horrible about yourself. It cuts off hope and keeps you bound to the past.

Many years ago, a young Midwestern lawyer suffered from such deep depression that his friends thought it wise to keep all knives and razors from him. During this time he wrote, "I am now the most miserable man living. Whether I shall ever be better, I cannot tell. I awfully forebode I shall not." He was wrong. This man did recover and went on to become one of America's most revered presidents, Abraham Lincoln.[5]

Our need for affirmation is as vital as our need for food. One way to satisfy this need is by surrounding ourselves with affirming, encouraging people—those who can cheer us up so that hope remains alive in our hearts. Dennis and Barbara Rainey write in *Building Your Mate's Self-Esteem,* "Words that communicate belief are important to your mate's self-image. He needs your unparalleled belief in him. You have been drafted to play on his team, to be the coach who believes in him, and to be the cheerleader who gives praise even when he loses. He needs you to be his biggest fan, not his sharpest critic."[6] Affirmation is the essential tool that encouragers use to zap you with the energy you need to climb out of the abyss of failure. It changes your perspective and motivates you to open yet another door of possibility.

## *Encouragers Change Your Perspective*

Imagine the world-renowned apostle and spiritual father of significant leaders such as Titus and Mark writing to encourage you to run the race ahead of you. Timothy could not help but have had his perspective changed because of Paul's affirmation!

Paul writes, "For this reason I remind you to fan into flame the gift of God, which is in you through the laying on of my hands. For God did not give us a spirit of timidity, but a spirit of power, of love and of self-discipline" (2 Timothy 1:6–7).

The thought of Paul, the gifted leader, making reference to Timothy's gifts must have given him the impetus to keep growing.

Now, I know that you don't have the apostle Paul sending you letters of encouragement today. But spiritual encouragement from lesser-known people can produce the same results. This is what prompted the great revivalist George Whitefield to become one of the first clergymen to enlist laymen in church service, thereby breaking down the rigid barrier between clergy and the laity in ministry. Whitefield noticed that people with great gifts were not putting them to use because they lacked the affirmation of the nobles and the titles of the accomplished. Though he didn't reject educated and ordained clergy, he emphasized piety and gifts over official sanction. Whitefield said, "What was needed were men truly converted, called, gifted, and living a godly life."[7]

Paul challenged Timothy to not allow timidity to deter him from pursuing his appointment with destiny. Discouragement makes one timid, hesitant to move forward. Therefore, Paul's intention was to help his son in the faith realize that God had given him a spirit of power, love, and self-discipline. These strong words were intended to change Timothy's outlook on his life and calling. He needed to see things from God's perspective, not from one of limited vision, depression, or hopelessness. Paul's words of motivation indicated that there was another perspective—one that was clear, focused, and bright. Once the embers of Timothy's gifts were fanned by words of encouragement into a roaring flame, a meaningful future awaited him.

## Encouragement is Gasoline for the Soul

Encouragers are the real leaders in life! They pick people up from the ash heap of depression, failure, and disillusionment, and set them firmly on a foundation of hope. Hope is the language of encouragers. Encouragers speak this language to ordinary and extraordinary people alike because they want them to live rich and rewarding lives.

My mother is a natural encourager. In my first year of college, I was taking calculus—a foundational class for all engineering students. Prior to that, I had never failed a class in my life. But calculus was giving me a hard time; I couldn't grasp the abstract mathematical concepts. I had sunk into a state of disillusionment because I thought I was sure to fail this class. In my embarrassment, I hadn't told anyone about my status in the class. One day I went to check my mailbox. To my surprise, there was a short, handwritten note from my mother. It read, "David, what men have done, men can do." When I read the note, I gained the necessary strength to conquer calculus. I passed the class with a "C." It wasn't the greatest grade in the world, but I overcame the temptation to give up. The deciding factor came when I read that note.

Last spring I went to the local nursery to purchase my summer annuals. I noticed one of the workers talking to herself as she watered the flowers. I was in a playful mood, so I said to her, "Are you talking to yourself?"

She said, "Yes, sometimes I'm the only one who will listen."

Her response made me chuckle, and I thought about the role of an encourager. Maybe you, like this woman, feel that there is a shortage of encouragers in your life. You look around and wonder if your situation is scaring off the encouragers. It's as if your case is so depressing that the encouragers are afraid to tackle it. Not so!

You've probably heard the silly story of the man who approached his doctor timidly and whispered, "Doctor, could you split my personality for me?"

"Split your personality? What on earth for?" the doctor asked.

The little man squirmed and said, "Oh, Doctor, I'm so lonesome!"

There are times when we need to encourage ourselves. I'm not suggesting that you walk around talking to yourself. If you choose to do that, it's your own business! My point is that there is a need for us to see ourselves as sources of our own victory. You encourage yourself by remembering the good times, thanking God for them, and acknowledging that He is the God of the second, third, and even the umpteenth chance!

Once when David was hiding in a cave because King Saul was trying to kill him, he wrote this verse: *"Look to my right and see; no one is concerned for me. I have no refuge; no one cares for my life"* (Psalm 142:4). David had learned to look to God—and not necessarily to people—for personal encouragement. This psalm was written as a prayer requesting divine involvement. It was never David's intention to write a song during his years of wandering. Rather, in a moment of personal contemplation before the Lord, this prayer flowed out of his life. Years later it became a song and was included by the Holy Spirit in sacred Scripture. You and I, along with millions of other people over the course of several thousands of years, have benefited from David's personal time of reflection and prayer. He became what he needed. David became his own encourager. Since no one was present to show the concern he needed, he encouraged himself. God has given you the internal fortitude to encourage yourself and others. Everyone is an encourager. We can all open windows of possibility and discover options that create momentum toward progress. Even if your natural disposition is negative, you can become an encourager. Both optimists and pessimists contribute to society. Proof? The optimist invents the airplane and the pessimist invents the parachute!

Growing as an encourager is vital. Not everyone will see your vision or how close you are to achieving it. Some may understand your dreams but try to discourage you from pursuing them. Consequently, you will have to master the art of self-encouragement. The biographies of many celebrated personalities reveal that they suffered painful discouragement from their teachers, parents, and peers. Many of them were told they would never make it or that they simply didn't have the necessary talent. But they wouldn't listen. They remained firm in following their own beliefs. Woody Allen, the Academy Award-winning writer, producer, and director, flunked motion picture production at New York University and the City College of New York. Malcolm Forbes, the late editor-in-chief of *Forbes* magazine, one of the largest business publications in the world, didn't make the staff of *The Princetonian*, the Princeton University newspaper.[8] These two men became giants in the very fields they flunked because they learned to encourage themselves.

The late Earl Nightingale, a writer and publisher of inspirational and motivational material, once told a story about a boy named Sparky. For Sparky, school was next to impossible. He failed every subject in the eighth grade. He flunked physics in high school, getting a grade of zero. Sparky also flunked Latin, algebra, and English. He didn't do much better at sports.

Throughout his youth, Sparky was awkward socially. He wasn't actually disliked by the other students; no one cared that much. Sparky was a loser. He, his classmates, everyone knew it. Sparky made up his mind early in life that he would content himself with what appeared to be his inevitable mediocrity. However, one thing was important to Sparky—drawing. He was proud of his artwork. In his senior year of high school, he submitted some cartoons to the editors of the year-book. The cartoons were turned down. Despite this particular rejection, Sparky was so convinced of his ability that he decided to become a professional artist. Later he sent samples of his work to Walt Disney Studios. Once again he was rejected.

Finally Sparky decided to write his autobiography in cartoons. He described his childhood as a loser and chronic underachiever. Sparky, the boy who'd had such a lack of success, was finally accepted. For Sparky, the boy whose work was rejected time and again, was Charles Schulz. He created the world-famous "Peanuts" comic strip, portraying himself as the famously unsuccessful character, Charlie Brown.[9] This true story proves once again that failure is written in pencil. Despite his many rejections and lack of encouragement, Charles Schulz learned to encourage himself.

The sad commentary is that many people go to their graves with unfulfilled dreams because they have no encouragers, nor do they know how to encourage themselves. One of the most secure jobs in life is that of an encourager. Encouragers are always needed. In every area of business, whether medicine, law, politics, or even waste management, encouragers are lacking. A friend who is the pastor of a large church mentioned recently that he had a staff person who was barely meeting the requirements of his job. Yet my friend could never fire this man because he was such a great encourager. Every time my friend was feeling discouraged, this particular staff person would come around and, with no prior knowledge, say just the right things to motivate him. The pastor said he had become so accustomed to this man's words of encouragement that he would often call him up just to say, "Please encourage me."

Do you want a job for life? Become an encourager! And stop living in denial concerning your own need for encouragement. Become discerning about the people God is placing around you as encouragers. Encouragers are everywhere, waiting to be recognized and appreciated. Encouragement is a gift!

# Chapter 7

# HE BIT
# HIS EAR!

*The difference between success and failure is that*
*successful people make themselves do what they hate to do*
*and failures wait for their managers to make them do it, or*
*to do it for them.*

—*Charlie "Tremendous" Jones*

To overcome painful obstacles, you must know how to hold on to your mission despite the pain you're feeling. Splashed across the front page of every major newspaper and on all the news programs was the report of the 1997 match between Mike Tyson and Evander Holyfield. In violation of the rules of the World Boxing Association (WBA), Mike Tyson was disqualified after Round 3 of the twelve-round WBA heavyweight championship fight for biting Holyfield on both his ears. Holyfield, the reigning champ, jumped up and down in pain, and the referee temporarily stopped the fight with thirty-three seconds remaining in the round. On his way back to the corner, Tyson shoved Holyfield from behind.

Evander Holyfield, a Christian, remained focused during Tyson's unprofessional attack, even while in excruciating pain. Once again a biblical principle was tried and proven in the crucible of modern life. The practice of self-restraint is an invaluable tool during times of disorder and confusion. Holyfield didn't retaliate against Tyson in a similarly destructive manner. He kept his composure before the world and defeated the contender without losing his cool or his Christian witness. But unlike the heavyweight champ, many people find it impossible to keep their cool during times of panic and confusion.

A less experienced boxer than Evander Holyfield might have retaliated in an unethical or even subversive way. The stake was not only the hefty purse of $30 million for each boxer, but also the world heavyweight title. Holyfield had a lot to lose. In the same way, your fight with failure is also a high-stakes match. Respond impulsively, and you'll be further away from your goals. There are three principles associated with Holyfield's actions that can help you win your battle with failure. First, you must become bigger than your pain. Second, growth comes from pain. And third, pain can keep you focused on your mission.

## You Are Bigger Than Your Pain

Although Evander Holyfield stands six feet, two inches tall and weighs 210 pounds of solid muscle, his internal fortitude—not his size—is what made him bigger than his pain. You may not have the physique of a heavyweight champ, but by drawing upon your spiritual strength you can face any circumstance that comes your way. Throughout history, obscure characters graced the center stage of life because they proved to be bigger than their pain. They made the right decisions amidst their discomfort, and their pain was somehow overshadowed. Their pain did not rule them; they ruled their pain.

### Round One: When It Rains, It Pours

Job, believed to be the oldest book in the Bible, records the trag-

114

edies and subsequent restoration of a man named Job. You cannot talk about the subject of pain and not include a discussion of Job—a man who faced almost every conceivable type of pain known. As the book of Job opens, Satan is seeking from God permission to try Job, to test his devotion to God. Job wasn't some ordinary guy in his day. In fact, the Bible describes him as the greatest man among all the people of the East (Job 1:3). This means that Job had financial power and influence. In addition, he was impeccable in his personal ethics and exemplary in his character before the Lord (Job 1:1). Satan's presupposition, however, was that Job only served God because his life was comfortable, both materially and relationally. If Job's wealth and family were removed, Satan believed Job would live a godless life. God granted Satan's request to strip Job of everything he had.

In one day, Satan destroyed Job's seven thousand sheep, three thousand camels, five hundred yoke of oxen, five hundred donkeys, and all of his servants (Job 1:13–17). Each of the four groups of animals represented a multimillion dollar enterprise. In the culture of that day, these animals were more than livestock on a farm. Sheep were shorn to provide wool. The wool was used to manufacture clothing. Job's business was the precursor of today's Nordstrom or Macy's clothing stores! Camels, in that day, were used for long distance travel. The reason Job had three thousand camels was because they were used to carry news to various destinations. Job had an international news business. He was the predecessor of today's CNN or AT&T! His five hundred yoke of oxen were used to plow the fields. A yoke of oxen represents two to six oxen. Thus, five hundred yoke of oxen equals conservatively one thousand oxen. These oxen were used to plow, till, and gather the food grown on thousands of acres of land. The harvested food would subsequently be sold in huge quantities. Job was the precursor of today's huge supermarket chains. The fourth enterprise Job conducted was with his five hundred donkeys. Women, children, and elderly men used donkeys for short distance travel. Even Jesus rode a donkey in His triumphal entry into Jerusalem as a sign of His humility (Zechariah 9:9). Job's enterprise with donkeys equated to what we know today as a taxicab or limousine service. In one solitary day, Job lost all of these lucrative, powerful businesses.

Before Job could mourn or weep over his loss, a messenger announced that his seven sons and three daughters were also killed (Job 1:18–19). Talk about bad news. Job heard more bad news in one day than most people experience in a lifetime. And most would not be able to survive a devastation of this magnitude. But not only did Job survive Satan's attack, he used it to show that he was bigger than his pain. Here's what Job said and did when the painful news was presented to him:

> *At this, Job got up and tore his robe and shaved his head.*
> *Then he fell to the ground in worship and said: Naked I*
> *came from my mother's womb, and naked I will depart. The*
> *LORD gave and the LORD has taken away; may the name of*
> *the LORD be praised.*
>
> —(Job 1:20–21)

Wow! What a man of God! Job recognized that his pain did not give him the right to assault the character of God. Job's perspective of his tragedy enabled him to jump quickly to the conclusion that God ought not be accused of an act of injustice. He didn't accuse God of behaving unrighteously. Job simply said, *"Naked I came from my mother's womb, and naked I will depart."* Job praised God for the opportunity to have experienced life and prosperity. Job removed himself from the temptation to sit in the judgment seat against God. Don't you wish you could do that? Don't worry—you'll get the opportunity! Perhaps you're living in that opportunity right now. Seize the moment and worship God for who He is and for His blameless ways. Although you may not know how your failure has occurred, God remains just in every one of His decisions and actions. Take a moment and spend some time on your knees, worshipping God as Job did. The Lord deserves it.

## Round Two: When It Pours, It Really Pours

Job's trial didn't stop there. When Satan saw that Job was unmoved by his painful losses, he made a second request of God. This time Satan said, *"A man will give all he has for his own life. But stretch out your hand and strike his flesh and bones, and he will surely curse you to your face"* (Job 2:4–5). God approved this request, and Satan afflicted Job with painful sores from the soles of his feet to the top of his head. Job's wife said to him, *"Are you still holding on to your integrity? Curse God and die"* (Job 2:9)! Her statement reflected her perspective that Job's situation was hopeless and that his ailments were incurable. *"He replied, 'You are talking like a foolish woman. Shall we accept good from God, and not trouble?' In all this, Job did not sin in what he said"* (Job 2:10).

This second assault on Job was so physically painful and psychologically discomforting that his wife advised him to abandon his personal ethics and curse God. But because Job's character was bigger than his pain, he rebuked his wife and kept honoring God in the midst of his trauma. Imagine suffering from incurable sores that were painful and itching. The irritation was so terrible that Job sat in ashes and scraped himself with a piece of broken pottery in an attempt to gain relief (Job 2:8).

In my estimation, Job's two-round match with Satan must have had a long-term effect on his emotional and physical conditions. But the positive results Job gained far outweighed the pain he experienced. Job became closer to the Lord through his season of pain. It is in our humiliation, grief, and trials that we really take the time to know and appreciate God. Worship during such times in our lives is not only therapeutic, but also necessary for spiritual survival.

The result of Satan's testing of Job is that God's initial opinion of Job proved to be true. *"There is no one on earth like him; he is blameless and upright, a man who fears God and shuns evil,"* God had told Satan. In the latter part of Job's life, God blessed him more than at the first. *"He had fourteen thousand sheep, six thousand camels, a thousand yoke of oxen and a thousand donkeys. And he also had seven sons and three daughters"* (Job 42:12–13). Job's life is an example of what our lives can be like. God bountifully rewards people who prove to be bigger than their pain.

### GROWTH COMES FROM PAIN!

Pain is an excellent teacher when viewed from the right perspective. It leads you to discover your true feelings, which are often concealed by shame and humiliation. The path to recovery—as well as the direction you choose to take in the future—is hidden behind these blinding emotions. Fierce battles must be fought on many fronts, including the psychological, if victory is to be realized.

Remember Evander Holyfield? His shame and humiliation were defeated because he maintained his integrity. Holyfield's actions showed that he believed he would not lose the fans' respect by not retaliating against Tyson. He was right! Because he chose to fight Tyson within the framework of the rules of boxing, the public placed him on an even higher pedestal as a champion boxer and as a man.

Similarly, Job received a commendation from God, and his integrity was recorded in the annals of sacred Scripture. In addition to blessing Job in the latter part of his life (Job 42:12), God testified of Job before his three friends: "My servant Job will pray for you [his friends], and I will accept his prayer and not deal with you according to your folly. You have not spoken of me what is right, as my servant Job has" (Job 42:8).

Before Job reached this pinnacle following his trial, he had to fight a fierce battle with disgrace and humiliation. Job's three friends came to comfort him in the midst of his pain. The first week of their visit was perfect. They simply sat on the ground with Job and said nothing. There is a strength that comes from silence—particularly the silence of close friends who will grieve with you during your pain. After a while, Job's friends, like most friends, felt they had the right to advise him about his crisis. Over the course of several days, each one of Job's friends gave him his perspective on the problem. The trio concluded that Job had been living in sin and that he was getting what he deserved from God. Job's friends also accused him of lying about his personal holiness and righteousness before the Lord.

Often we allow other people or our overactive imaginations to force us into unnecessary battles. The spectacle of your trial or failure may spawn unsolicited negative opinions about how you got into your situation. For awhile, Job debated with his friends the nature, wisdom, and sovereignty of God. But when he resolved to stop trying to figure out the mysteries of God, he was able to achieve growth from his pain.

When you're hurting, the temptation to try to figure out God can easily arise. Why God allowed this failure to befall you is the $64,000 question! Growth comes when you dismiss the question. There are some things you and I will never know while we live in these mortal bodies. Even if we could find out why God allows our failures, we wouldn't have the wisdom to understand or sort through the data. Assuming we had the intelligence to understand God's mysteries, we'd likely disagree with His approach or His reasoning. God is God, all by Himself. He doesn't need you or me to assist Him in the formulation of His divine plans. The moment you decide that you're not capable of aiding God is the moment growth begins to occur.

Job shut down his friends' foolish reasoning when he said, "The Almighty is beyond our reach and exalted in power; in his justice and great righteousness, he does not oppress" (Job 37:23). You must arrive at the same conclusion in the midst of your Job experience. You don't have the answers to your questions, so why not stop asking them? Growth comes from peace—peace of heart and peace of mind. Put away the high-minded, philosophical reasoning that won't get you anywhere anyway! You may never know why your divorce occurred, why your child died, why you lost that great job, or why you hurt the way you do. True maturity is not in knowing all the answers to your questions, but in enjoying life and God in the midst of your uncertainties.

## PAIN KEEPS YOU FOCUSED

In the appendix to C.S. Lewis' *The Problem of Pain,* R. Harvard wrote:

> Mental pain is less dramatic than physical pain, but it is more common and also more hard to bear. The frequent attempt to conceal mental pain increases the burden: it is easier to say "My tooth is aching" than to say "My heart is broken." Yet if the cause is accepted and faced, the conflict will strengthen and purify the character, and in time the pain

will usually pass. Sometimes, however, it persists and the effect is devastating; if the cause is not faced or not recognised, it produces the dreary state of the chronic neurotic. But some by heroism overcome even chronic mental pain. They often produce brilliant work and strengthen, harden, and sharpen their characters till they become like tempered steel.[1]

What a tremendous observation! Mental pain produces a sharpened character. This tells me that the sufferer becomes clearer in his mission and focus because of his battle with his pain. Every failure will teach you a lesson if you're open and willing to learn. Pain can be a blessing in disguise if your perspective is keen. "Spiritual truth is learned by atmosphere, not by intellectual reasoning," wrote Oswald Chambers. "God's Spirit alters the atmosphere of our way of looking at things, and things begin to be possible which never were possible before. Getting into the stride of God means nothing less than union with Himself. It takes a long time to get there, but keep at it. Don't give in because the pain is bad just now, get on with it, and before long you will find you have a new vision and a new purpose."[2]

Paul wrote, "I consider that our present sufferings are not worth comparing with the glory that will be revealed in us" (Romans 8:18). Paul was ultimately speaking about an eternal reward and the life hereafter. Yet there is an underlying message in the text. As a person grows in Christ, there is a glory that unfolds in and around him as a result of his victories through suffering. Suffering aids the child of God in yielding to the greater purposes of God and to His cultivation of character deep within. Paul chose to use the word *revealed,* which is the Greek word *apokalupto,* meaning "to take off the cover, or to disclose." This definition underscores the reality of the ongoing maturation process in the life of the Christian, particularly the maturation that occurs through pain and suffering. Actually, the benefit of maturation is available to anyone, Christian or non-Christian, who takes the time to adjust his perspective to a higher level of thinking.

This higher plane of living is one that allows you to gain a clearer focus on life. It allows you to grasp the divine plan for your life. Then you must decide what you're going to do with that plan. Either you'll take the low road—on which you'll complain about your situation, your pain, your discomfort, and the futility of your situation—or you'll take the high road, which offers hope, a clearer vision, and the peaceful assurance that you're following a divine plan. Although the high road may seem like an excruciatingly long way to your destination, with God as your life's traffic director, you will arrive right on time.

Job's suffering helped him live with a principle-centered mind-set. Job lived by principle, keeping eternity in his focus, rather than living for temporal blessings alone. In the broad scheme of things, how does your pain hold up in light of eternity? Will it be important one hundred years— even ten years—from now? When eternity is kept in mind, we can adopt and maintain the needed perspective during times of pain or crisis. Perspective makes all the difference in the world. In fact, perspective is reality. How you view things dictates your behavior, emotions, and conduct. So you must labor to see your life through the lens of eternity.

One day a grandfather was asked to watch his two little grandchildren while their mother went shopping. That afternoon, he took a short nap. The grandkids were extremely active and mischievous. As the grandfather napped, they decided to comb some Limburger cheese into his bushy mustache. When he awoke, he said to himself, "Something smells in this room." He walked into the living room, sniffing around. Soon he said, "Something stinks in here, too." He went outside and stood on the front porch. Then he announced loudly, "Something stinks out here! The whole world stinks!"

Perspective shapes your outlook on every area of life—even on people. One day a man was looking everywhere for his hedge cutter, but to no avail. Then he spotted his next-door neighbor's teenage son riding his bike. The boy looked like a thief to this man, and the man remembered that the boy even walked like a thief. "Surely he must have stolen my hedge cutter," thought the man. As he got ready to go next door and accuse the boy of the crime, he saw his hedge cutter near the back of the garage. Now when he looked across his fence at the teenager, the boy looked so innocent and well-mannered. "A fine boy," thought the man to himself. See how perspective shaped his behavior and thoughts of others?

Most of us collapse at the first pang of pain. We fall down on the threshold of God's purpose and languish in self-pity. And the well-intentioned sympathy of all our Christian friends will only hasten our demise. But God will not. He comes with the grip of the pierced hand of His Son and says, "Enter into fellowship with Me; arise and shine." If through a broken heart God can bring His purposes to pass in the world, then thank Him for breaking your heart.[3]

As we draw closer to Christ, our pain will be used by Him to keep us focused on eternity. Pain is our servant, not our master. Use it for your gain. Use it for your benefit. Use it for your ministry. In the words of Thomas á Kempis, "Besides, the more the flesh is distressed by affliction, so much the more is the spirit strengthened by inward grace. Not infrequently a man is so strengthened by his love of trials and hardship in his desire to conform to the cross of Christ, that he does not wish to be without sorrow or pain, since he believes he will be the more acceptable to God if he is able to endure more and more grievous things for His sake."[4]

## A Look at the Unjust Judge

Jesus used parables—earthly stories with heavenly meanings—to teach his disciples principles of kingdom living. One such story was the parable of the persistent widow. The Lord used this story to help His followers understand how they must behave when faced with apparent defeat or mental pain. Listen to the words of Jesus:

> [2]"*In a certain town there was a judge who neither feared God nor cared about men.* [3]*And there was a widow in that town who kept coming to him with the plea, 'Grant me justice against my adversary.' *[4]*For some time he refused. But finally he said to himself, 'Even though I don't fear God or care about men, *[5]*yet because this widow keeps bothering me, I will see that she gets justice, so that she won't eventually wear me out with her coming!'*
> [6]*...Listen to what the unjust judge says. *[7]*And will not God bring about justice for his chosen ones, who cry out to him day and night? Will he keep putting them off? *[8]*I tell you, he will see that they get justice, and quickly. However, when the Son of Man comes, will he find faith on the earth?*"
> —(Luke 18:2–8)

### *Excuses Must Be Discarded*

In ancient Palestine, there were no advocates for the elderly, the poor, or common citizens. Everyone was on his own. Bribery would have been the typical method of winning a case for a woman in this position. Apparently the widow's case was money related. New Testament Greek scholar Joachim Jeremias writes, "Since the widow brings her case to a single judge, and not before a tribunal, it would appear to be a money-matter: a debt, a pledge, or a portion of an inheritance, is being withheld from her.[5] Quite obviously, the widow was experiencing a degree of emotional pain related to her financial problem. The discomfort was so severe that she needed a judge's ruling and enforcement to gain relief from her adversary.

The widow did not allow politeness to hinder her from pleading her case, even though her pleas were bothersome to the judge. In fact, the judge granted her justice just because she was irking him! The woman discarded the excuses that she was female, a widow, poor, and a commoner. She faced one of the most powerful men in her town and moved him to give her justice. Failure always overtakes those who lack the will to act. This widow refused to be limited by a bunch of excuses. She needed justice. There was no other option. Her voice had to be heard.

What was Jesus trying to teach His disciples through this simple story? Most scholars agree that the story is about both the widow and the judge. The judge, a man with considerable authority, was blinded by his power. He neither feared God nor heeded the cries of the poor. Yet when a defenseless widow, a victim of injustice and exploitation, made up her mind, nothing was able to stop her.

This is Jesus' point. Through your pain, you are being taught by the Master Teacher to never give up, despite what your circumstances look like. Pain can fuel you to gain powerful victories. True success is first gained internally. It is exhibited by your determination to not give up. Conversely, true failure first occurs on the inside, when you throw in the towel. This widow plowed through the mental, social, and physical deterrents to plead and win her case. If such an unjust judge will honor perseverance, think how much more a loving God will hear and respond to our pleas for help!

*Why Didn't the Widow Quit?*

A true fighter never gives up, regardless of the challenge. Jesus posed the question, *"Will not God bring about justice for his chosen ones, who cry out to him day and night?"* (Luke 18:7). He answered this rhetorical question with a strong affirmative statement: *"I tell you, he will see that they get justice, and quickly"* (Luke 18:8). The widow didn't quit fighting because her adversary's injustice was too painful to disregard. Moreover, this widow was determined that she would not become a victim of circumstances. The successful outcome of her case would also help others to rise beyond the status quo or the limits imposed by their social status. New Testament professor John Donahue makes the following observation:

> She shatters convention by going alone and directly confronting the judge; she is publicly persistent in demanding her rights, and the imagery from one of the more violent athletic contests (boxing) shatters the stereotype of the vulnerable widow. The hearers are confronted with a new vision of reality, inaugurated by God's reign, where victims will claim their rights and seek justice—often in an unsettling manner.[6]

Everyone was shocked by the woman's persistence, because as a widow, she was one of the lowest people on the social ladder. Despite public opinion, she did not quit. Her frequent pleas to the judge showed that she was not going to take a position of indifference.

Most people will become indifferent after a first or second refusal. Indifference is failure. Upon receiving the Nobel Peace Prize in 1986, Elie Wiesel challenged an audience, "Take sides. Neutrality helps

126

the oppressor, never the victim. Silence encourages the tormentor, never the tormented." We too must be willing to take a stand. A failure is a person who has blundered and is not able to reap the benefits of the experience. The widow's actions reveal that her heart was unwilling to settle for failure in the matter. She wanted to conquer her pain by winning justice over her unnamed adversary. Consequently, each refusal by the judge was met with another appointment to plead her case. "A complacent and fearless judge is pummeled like a faltering boxer by a woman fighting for her rights," Donahue concludes.[7]

There are many ways to become a failure. But by never taking a chance, you're guaranteed to succeed as a failure. This widow kept up the pressure until justice was served. She used her pain to fuel her eventual relief. We too must petition God for relief and justice. In this story, as in many others, Jesus confronted the passive, *laissez-faire* attitude many people take regarding their destinies. God wants you to come to Him, draw close to Him, and by faith, gain your healing, deliverance, and personal victory through your persistence toward Him.

## *Fighters Don't Know How to Quit!*

Someone once said, "Don't worry about what's ahead. Just go as far as you can go; from there you can see farther." How true! This statement is just another way of saying "We walk by faith, not by sight." Fighters don't know how to quit. They breathe faith. In the face of pain, failure, and adversity, fighters keep going.

An athlete was once blinded in a freak boxing accident. The doctors told him he'd never see again. The social workers told him to learn Braille, stay at home, and accept the fact that he'd be dependent on others for the rest of his life. But the boxer, Morris Frank, fought to regain his independence. The result was the development of The Seeing Eye, the organization that trains Seeing-Eye™ dogs for the blind.[8] Fighters are fighters, whether they're dealing with the tough issues of life or trying to attain the goals they've established.

The California coast was shrouded in fog the morning of July 4, 1952. Twenty-one miles to the west, on Catalina Island, a thirty-four-year-old woman waded into the water and began swimming to California, determined to be the first woman to do so. Her name was Florence Chadwick, and she had already been the first woman to swim the English Channel in each direction. The water was numbingly cold that morning, and the fog so thick she could hardly see the boats in her party. Several times, sharks had to be driven away with rifles to protect the lone figure in the water. As the hours ticked off, Chadwick swam on. Fatigue had never been her problem on these swims; it was the bone-chilling cold of the water.

More than fifteen hours later, numbed by the cold, she asked to be pulled out of the water. She couldn't go on, she said. Millions were watching on national television, as both her mother and her trainer, alongside her in the boat, told her she was near land. They urged her not to quit. But when Chadwick looked toward the California coast, all she could see was dense fog. Later, Florence Chadwick reflected that she had almost given up just a half mile from the California coast! She had nearly been licked, not by fatigue or even cold; the fog had nearly defeated her because it obscured her goal.

It was the only time Florence Chadwick ever quit. Two months later she swam that same channel, and again fog obscured her view. But this time she swam with her faith intact; somewhere behind that fog was the land. Not only was she the first woman to swim the Catalina Channel, but she also beat the men's record by some two hours![9]

The widow in Jesus' parable was adamant about her need for justice. She knew that her only obstacle was getting through to the judge. Archibald Hunter writes, "If even a man with so many reasons for being disobliging, runs the argument, can be moved to give you what you ask, how much more will God lend a ready ear to his children's requests."[10] The Bible is full of encouragement that there's a spot in the winner's circle for you, if your faith fails not. Many of life's failures are people who didn't realize how close they were to success when they gave up. Fighters never quit. You're a fighter! Don't quit!

# —— Chapter 8 ——

# OKAY,
# COACH!

*For all of us who fail at one thing or another, take heart in
one fact. In baseball, you can fail two out of three times at
the plate and still make a few million dollars a year.*
*—Author Unknown*

The house where I grew up was located across the street from a large park with four baseball fields. You can imagine how I spent my summers. From the time I was eight years old, I played baseball eight hours a day. Every summer, my Dad registered my brothers and me in the local baseball league. Our first summer in the league, I didn't know one end of the bat from the other. My coach taught me what to do, and he dealt with each player according to his need—not only in learning baseball, but in life.

Some players needed an older brother, while others needed a father figure; some of us needed a counselor, yet others needed a baseball expert who took a personal interest in developing their talents. The coach wore a different hat with each player. The more the team developed a mind-set of playing to win, the more these unique relationships were needed to serve the overall purpose of the team. I began to realize that my baseball coach was becoming a life-management specialist to us. He addressed the areas of our lives that were lacking, areas where we needed special instruction from someone who had already traveled the road we were now traveling. Now, I'm sure our coach got more than he bargained for when he volunteered to coach Little League baseball! Quite obviously, he was not the most experienced life-management specialist, but he was all we had. And since we were only boys, we didn't know whether our coach was doing a good job or not. In our eyes, he was the man. He was our coach, and we would defend him before the world if need be.

Because I developed a love for the game, it turns out that I've had many baseball coaches throughout my lifetime. In high school, in semi-professional leagues, and in college, I ran across all types of coaches—some good, some bad; some weak, some strong; some caring, and some who couldn't care less. But regardless of his disposition, the coach was always an invaluable asset to the team. I learned that whether I had a winning team or a losing team depended greatly on the coach. Similarly, I saw that in life, success rises and falls on who your coach is.

American culture has produced a society that says "I can do it by myself! I really don't need anyone else." People today, including Christians, are generally less familiar with the precise roles of coaches, mentors, and role models. In sports, there are often multiple levels of coaches for a single team. For example, in professional baseball, you have the general coach, the batting coach, the fielding coach, the running coach, and the pitching coach. They are all specialists in their respective areas. Each one brings a lifetime of experience to the table for the sole purpose of helping the team and its members fulfill their potentials. Yet in life, you rarely see people who are guided by mentors through life's awkward turns.

The world's greatest musicians play under the direction of a conductor—a coach, in a sense. These classical musicians, some having begun training as early as age six, willingly submit to the leadership of their conductor. This is because they know that as good as they are, the conductor can bring new levels of skill and a better performance out of them. The orchestra's "coach" sees untapped potential that the performers cannot see. The expert's opinion is invaluable.

Mentoring is a one-on-one (or small group) relationship between a mentor and a protégé for the development of a specific skill or art. A favorite mentoring story of mine is about a young pianist who came to Leonard Bernstein and asked to be mentored by him. Bernstein said, "Tell me what you want to do, and I will tell you whether or not you're doing it." Bernstein essentially said to the young man, "You're responsible for your playing and your practice. The one thing you can't do is hear yourself as a great conductor hears you."

## THE ROLE OF A COACH

Coaching isn't just a science; it's an art. Much of it is subjective. Much of it is done because it just feels right. Try to explain how to coach, and you'll be lost for words. Try to convince the uninitiated or unschooled of the reasons for your decisions, and he'll walk away scratching his head because he just won't get it. And it's possible that he'll never get it. A mentor or a coach has almost a sixth sense—a gut feeling and a sensitivity to his protégé. Good coaches feel deeply. They are passionate about their jobs, their teams, and their players. They coach because they love to do it. It makes their adrenaline flow and presses all the right buttons in them. Mentoring is their reason for being. It's what they live for—to assist others in becoming champions.

A mentor sees his protégé's potential and works feverishly to get him to his highest level of skill. Consider two caterpillars crawling across the grass. They notice a butterfly flying over them. One nudges the other and says, "You couldn't get me up in one of those things for a million dollars!" Protégés, like these caterpillars, don't necessarily see that one day they will be butterflies—champions. But their coaches see what they are capable of doing and labor to assist them in living up to their potential.

One evening while a man was driving down a country road, he lost control of his car and wound up in a ditch. He walked to the closest farmhouse and asked for help pulling the car out. The farmer said, "Sure. Let me hitch up Dusty, and you'll be out in no time."

A few minutes later the farmer appeared with Dusty—an old, sway-backed, nearly blind mule. After Dusty was hitched to the car, the farmer cracked the whip and said, "Pull, Buck, pull." Nothing happened. The farmer cracked the whip again and said, "Pull, Clyde, pull." Nothing happened. He cracked the whip again and said, "Pull, Dusty, pull." Dusty began to pull, until finally the car was out of the ditch.

The man thanked the farmer, then said, "But I'm really curious. If your mule's name is Dusty, why did you say 'Pull, Buck' and 'Pull, Clyde'?"

The farmer said, "Well, you know, Dusty's old and he doesn't see too good, and he doesn't have much confidence. If he thought he had to do all the work himself, he'd never even try."

Coaches are like this farmer, and protégés are like old Dusty. Dusty didn't realize his potential apart from the farmer's assistance. In the New Testament, we learn that we have unlimited potential. John wrote, *"Dear friends, now we are children of God, and what we will be has not yet been made known. But we know that when he [Jesus] appears we shall be like him, for we shall see him as he is"* (1 John 3:2). God has created you with significant potential. The goal is to live up to it. And a coach can aid you in achieving this God-designed goal.

## The Mentor Must Believe in the Protégé's Potential

It's hard to find people who genuinely believe in you. When you find such a person, don't be too quick to dissolve that relationship! A good life-management specialist is someone you'll want to keep as an asset in your life. Success is more easily attained if the people we let into our lives know how to help us manage failure. You need a coach—a person who believes in you—to help you manage your experiences of failure. One way a mentor can help is simply by affirming you.

"I'm really worried," said one little boy to a friend. "Dad slaves away at his job so I'll never want for anything, so I'll be able to go to college if I want to. Mom works hard every day washing and ironing, cleaning up after me, taking care of me when I get sick. They spend every day of their lives working on my behalf. I'm worried."

His friend asked, "What have you got to worry about?"

The first boy replied, "I'm afraid they might try to escape!"[1]

This boy understood the value of his parents. Similarly, protégés must recognize the need for coaches who make invaluable contributions to their lives just by their dependable actions. In the busy world in which we live, your coach may not necessarily see you every week or every month, yet his or her priceless advice and friendship should be sought out and valued.

Seeing someone else's potential is a very difficult thing to do, especially if he's in the middle of a painful and confusing time. A coach, however, isn't afraid of getting his hands dirty. He just wants to know that his protégé is worth the investment of his time, counsel, and wealth of knowledge. A person who is dealing with failure isn't likely to be thinking as clearly as he normally would. A good coach will realize this and may endure a lot of unnecessary headaches because he's willing to work through the pain of failure to guide his protégé to a brighter future.

A teenage girl became increasingly rebellious after her parents' divorce. Late one night, the police called her mother down to the police station to pick her up. She had been arrested for drunken driving. The distraught mother and angry daughter didn't speak until the next afternoon. Finally the mother broke the tension by giving her daughter a small, gift-wrapped box. The daughter nonchalantly opened it and found a small rock inside. She rolled her eyes and said, "Cute, Mom. What's this for?"

"Here's the card," the mother said. Her daughter took the card out of the envelope and read it. Tears started to trickle down her cheeks. She got up and gave her mom a big hug as the card fell to the floor. On the card were these words: "This rock is more than two hundred million years old. That's how long it will take before I give up on you."[2]

Failure tends to isolate its victim, cutting him off from friends and family. As a protégé, you must make the conscious choice to open up your life, your struggles, and even your failures, to keep the right people aware of your needs. Our society is not so corrupt that all of its coaches have been eliminated. A failure-management specialist, however, will want to see vulnerability and sincerity on the part of a potential protégé, before he will extend a helping hand. If these character traits are not present, a mentor may not be willing to invest the time. There are innumerable people who want to be mentored by someone who cares. Many potential protégés, however, are not serious about changing. These disqualify themselves because they are stubbornly set in their ways. Coaches must be selective about whom they mentor.

## *A Mentor Helps Define the Vision, Goal, and Plan*

Wisdom is the number one qualification for leadership. Wisdom provides insight, foresight, and at times, even hindsight. This is why James wrote, "Who is wise and understanding among you? Let him show it by his good life, by deeds done in the humility that comes from wisdom" (James 3:13). This passage establishes a requirement for spiritual leaders. Mentors cannot take their protégés where they themselves have not gone. This includes the development of qualities such as moral character, high ethical standards, discipline, and honesty. What good is it to climb the ladder of success, only to reach the top and realize that the ladder was leaning against the wrong building? Mentors help to define the goals and plans of those they mentor. No, they don't try to change their protégés' dreams and goals. They help clarify them by determining whether a match exists between the gifts of the protégé and the goal he is aspiring to.

A protégé may be gifted in many areas, and his greatest dilemma may be in choosing which area to pursue as his life's work. "When I was a boy, my father, a baker, introduced me to the wonders of song," related Luciano Pavarotti. "He urged me to work very hard to develop my voice. Arrigo Pola, a professional tenor in my hometown of Modena, Italy, took me as a pupil. I also enrolled in a teachers' college. On graduating, I asked my father, 'Shall I be a teacher or a singer?' 'Luciano,' my father replied, 'if you try to sit on two chairs, you will fall between them. For life, you must choose one chair.'" Luciano chose one. It took seven years of study and frustration before he made his first professional appearance. It took another seven years to reach the Metropolitan Opera. Luciano concluded, "Whether it's laying bricks, writing a book—whatever we choose—we should give ourselves to it.

137

Commitment, that's the key. Choose one chair."

Mentors provide the kind of input and guidance that Pavarotti's dad gave him at that critical juncture in his life. Had the uncertainty of his career path been allowed to linger in Pavarotti's mind, the world may have been denied the gift of his great talent. Although Pavarotti's father was a small-town baker, his words were those of a world-class mentor. You don't need the president of the United States to mentor you, just a caring person who has foresight about your life.

Once the vision for your life is clear, a plan must be developed. Remember, the vision must be an accurate reflection of your abilities and gifts. Picture our old friend Charlie Brown at bat. Having just struck out (again!), he slumps over to the bench. "Rats!" he exclaims. "I'll never be a big-league player. I just don't have it! All my life I've dreamed of playing in the big leagues, but I know I'll never make it."

Lucy turns to console him. "Charlie Brown, you're thinking too far ahead. What you need to do is set yourself more immediate goals."

Charlie Brown looks up. "Immediate goals?"

"Yes," Lucy replies. "Start with this next inning when you go out to pitch. See if you can walk out to the pitcher's mound without falling down!"

If your purpose in life doesn't match your gifts, no amount of goal setting or strategic planning will help you achieve your dream. The mentor's job is to give direction to your plans. He or she will ask you pertinent questions about your plans, and may play devil's advocate in helping you identify the potential pitfalls of your goal.

In formulating a mentoring program for his children and grandchildren, Bobb Biehl, president of Masterplanning Group International, made these observations:

I made a list of pressures, temptations, and threats that our children and grandchildren will face. And it was a long list. I'm sure you could create a similar one. Most of the items on my list were things my generation did not even think about until we were in our twenties. But most of our children and grandchildren will see them portrayed, modeled, and even encouraged in real life or in living color on television and movie screens before they reach high school.[3]

As a mentor, Bobb Biehl realistically anticipated some of the struggles his children and grandchildren would experience in pursuit of their dreams. A mentor's foresight is priceless. Mentors think of things that their protégés will never even dream of. This is why they are so valuable. Given the right advice and perspective, your present challenges with failure could disappear. Begin to look around at the people you know, to see whether a mentoring relationship is possible. If you find no one suitable, ask your pastor or a local minister for the name of someone—perhaps an older man or woman—who would be willing to invest some time in the life of another person. Whatever you need is probably right in your midst. God would never tease us by giving us a compelling vision and then withholding the necessary resources to accomplish our dreams.

## THE ROLE OF A PROTÉGÉ

I recently began a mentoring program in my church. I chose thirty people who I thought showed considerable promise in handling significant leadership responsibilities at the church. I then sent out a memo asking each candidate whether he or she was interested in participating in a mentoring program. I listed several criteria each protégé would have to meet and maintain if he chose to accept my offer. For example:

1. A protégé should always be in the business of character development;
2. A protégé must be able to be held accountable by his mentor;
3. A protégé should demonstrate climbs and plateaus throughout the mentoring process.

The other requirements listed in my memo dealt with church-related items such as consistency in attendance, tithing, and effectiveness in handling ministry responsibility. My memo also indicated that those who accepted must understand and agree that they could be dismissed at any time if they did not meet the requirements. As you can see, I take mentoring very seriously. It requires a sacrifice for me as the mentor, as well as for the members of the group. Mentoring requires a serious and sober commitment by both the mentor and the protégé.

## *A Protégé Should Be in the Business of Character Development*

Oftentimes we are the last ones to know our own faults. It's like having bad breath. We don't know we have it until someone finally offers us a breath mint. Even then, we may ignorantly say "No, thank you" to the offer. The success of any person is largely based on how well he knows himself. All the encouragement in the world will not be profitable if you are unable to probe within and discern your motives, feelings, and ideas. You must be acutely aware of your own strengths and weaknesses.

Little Billy went to his mother demanding a new bicycle. His mother decided that Billy needed to take a look at himself and the way he was acting. She said, "Well, Billy, it isn't Christmas and we don't have the money to go out and buy you anything you want. So why don't you write a letter to Jesus and pray for one instead."

After his usual temper tantrum, Billy went to his room. He finally sat down to write a letter to Jesus:

Dear Jesus, I've been a good boy this year and would appreciate a new bicycle. Your friend, Billy.

Now, Billy knew that Jesus already knew what kind of boy he was—a brat! So he ripped up the letter and gave it another try:

Dear Jesus, I've been an okay boy this year and I want a new bicycle. Yours truly, Billy.

Well, Billy knew this letter wasn't totally honest either, so he tore it up and tried again:

Dear Jesus, I've thought about being a good boy this year and can I have a new bicycle? Billy.

Well, Billy looked deep down in his heart, which was what his mother really wanted him to do. He crumpled up the letter, threw it in the trash can and went running outside. He aimlessly wandered about. Depressed because of the way he had treated his parents, Billy seriously considered his actions. He found himself in front of a Catholic church. Billy went inside and knelt beside a pew. Looking around, unsure of what to do next, Billy finally got up to leave. Then he noticed the beautiful statues that graced the sanctuary. All of a sudden, he grabbed a small statue and ran out the door with it.

He went home, hid it under his bed, and wrote this letter:

Jesus, I've broken most of the Ten Commandments, shot spit wads in school, tore up my sister's Barbie doll, and lots more. I'm desperate. I've got your mama. If you ever want to see her again, give me a bike. Signed, You know who.

If you're going to rise above your failure with the help of a coach, character development must become your business. God can never take you beyond the level of your character. Just think for a moment about all the men and women in our generation who came tumbling down from the heights of their careers because they never made character development one of their personal ambitions. I can remember President Nixon and the Watergate scandal, the evangelist Jimmy Swaggart and his inappropriate relationships with prostitutes, Jim Bakker and the financial misdealings of PTL—and what about President Bill Clinton and the Monica Lewinsky matter? The list is endless. Wise decisions may cause you to get to the top, but solid character will allow you to stay there.

Character development requires that you take an honest assessment of yourself. It calls for you to accept the truth about who you are. Paul wrote, *"But if we judged ourselves, we would not come under judgment"* (1 Corinthians 11:31). A commitment to the growth of your character means that you judge yourself before anyone else has a chance to correct you. This doesn't mean that you are exempt from correction from others; it simply means that you're aware of your shortcomings and willing to do something about them.

Knowing your faults and not addressing them means that you lack the personal discipline to correct your problem. If procrastination is how you choose to handle a problem, the problem will eventually become more public. God's love for you and His desire for your success require that He correct you. *"When we are judged by the Lord, we are being disciplined so that we will not be condemned with the world,"* wrote Paul (1 Corinthians 11:32). This Scripture warns us that God is going to address our character development one way or another. If you move to correct the problem, great! If you drag your feet, then your procrastination is an open invitation for God to chasten you. The wisest approach is to address your issues as quickly as possible, without getting God involved.

One of my mentors, Dr. Kirby Clements, has aided me immensely by helping me see myself. This is not always pleasant because at times a painful subject must be broached over and over again until I realize and accept the truth of his observations. For example, Dr. Clements talked to me repeatedly about how I viewed my subordinates in ministry.

Before his intervening, my attitude was one of extreme impatience with staff members and leaders because of their inability to be as productive as I thought they could be. Unbeknownst to me, my frustration was reaching an unpleasant level. I was beginning to think that my subordinates were holding me back from achieving my potential and destiny. Kirby continued to hammer away at the issue. Initially, I insisted that I was right. He patiently kept up the pressure, debating with me and trying to convince me to adopt a more positive perspective. In one conversation he said, "David, if you were more affirming and encouraging of your leaders, you would get greater productivity out of them." With that comment, I finally heeded his advice. I began adjusting my perspective. Dr. Clements' mentoring relationship has helped hone my character to a higher level of godliness.

## *A Protégé Is to Be Accountable*

Accountability is a safety net of life. It will keep you anchored to a secure foundation during times of turbulence. Accountability deals largely with your character, and more specifically, with your behavior. Its purpose is preventive. Since your thoughts, behavior, feelings, and temptations all affect the attainability of your dreams, these areas should be guarded like a bank vault.

Many people believe that they have accountability in their lives. However, under intense scrutiny, their accountability relationships fall short of the true meaning of the word. Having accountability means living in a glass house before your mentor and before the world. As a pastor, I know firsthand what living in a glass house means! Others are constantly investigating my life—even people I don't know.

Over the past several years, our church has gained regional notoriety and experienced increased success because of our growth and the visibility of our weekly television program. Nowadays, I rarely go unnoticed at a mall or a large social event. This kind of attention, however, has its price. I have to be more conscious of how my actions may be interpreted by others. Recently, I was standing in line at the bank, waiting to make a few transactions. It was summertime on a Friday afternoon, and the line was exceptionally long. People began complaining because the line was not moving quickly enough. I didn't say anything. A week later someone came up to me in church and said, "I was in that bank with you last week, and I wanted to see how you would handle the frustration. That's why I didn't come over to you and say hello."

Accountability means that your life is an open book to your mentor at all times. He or she can pose questions about your behavior for any reason. Becoming a protégé means that you want your life to be lived out in the best possible way. This means that purity is the standard you seek to live by.

## *A Protégé Should Demonstrate Climbs and Plateaus*

Every mentoring relationship should have a set purpose. Sometimes a mentor is needed simply because you sense that your life has reached a plateau in personal, spiritual, vocational, or even ministry-related development. Thus, the mentor's wisdom is sought for a specific goal. Paul Stanley and J. Robert Clinton, in their book *Connecting,* write, "Mentoring is a relational process in which a mentor, who knows or has experienced something, transfers that something (resources of wisdom, information, experience, confidence, insight, relationships, status, etc.) to a mentoree, at an appropriate time and manner, so that it facilitates development or empowerment."[4] Mentors are to transfer something to their protégés. Once this resource or development skill is received, the mentoring relationship ceases. Although mentoring is for life, individual mentoring relationships cease once their purposes have been served.

Mentors want to know that their mentorees are growing and developing in the areas they contribute to. Therefore, a protégé should demonstrate climbs and plateaus throughout the relationship. Mentoring someone in an area such as leadership can be very subjective. It may be difficult to determine whether growth has been achieved. Although the stages of growth can be established by studying various leadership models, the response of each protégé will be unique. If the relationship is healthy and the mentor has something significant to offer, personal development of the protégé is sure to occur.

I played baseball in college. My coach recommended that I practice with the track team for about a month until my speed improved. I had always been a slow runner throughout my baseball career. However, this coach determined that my speed could be enhanced by performing speed drills, which have proven to be quite successful with track runners. The next afternoon I was practicing with the track stars.

The track coach gave me a number of drills that included sprints, hurdles, and stretching. After about a month, my speed improved noticeably. At that point, I was no longer required to practice with the track team.

Similarly, our failure-management coaches or mentors may demand to see progress in specific areas. After achieving a growth spurt, you will normally level off or experience a plateau for an undetermined period of time. The plateau serves you by allowing you to assimilate the new knowledge and experiences you've gained during the growth phase. The cycle of growth/plateau continues throughout the mentoring program, as well as throughout life.

Mentors and protégés are meant for one another. Coaches and players are inseparable twins, joined at the hip. Likewise, a person experiencing failure needs a failure-management specialist. This type of coach is simply an ordinary, caring person who has either gone through what you are going through or who has a lot of wisdom. Pray to the Lord right now, and ask Him to bring this kind of a person into your life. Life on earth is brief. Seize the opportunity. Begin looking around, because a failure-management coach may already be in your life, just waiting for your personal invitation to begin the process. Go ahead—invite him or her to mentor you through your present crisis. It will prove to be invaluable.

## THE ROLE OF HARD WORK

Successful people work hard—contrary to the late-night infomercials showing how you can own your own real estate empire without working, or how you can lose weight without proper diet and exercise. Those lies don't work. They present false hope and false security, and they undermine God's philosophy of personal advancement through a biblical work ethic. Hard work, hard work, hard work is the way you climb to the top. Hard work, however, does not guarantee success. Working hard and working smart can assure you of quality results. Working smart means adopting traits such as integrity, the foresight to plan, and a sensitivity to people's needs.

A minister who used to be lazy shared this praise report on how he became a hard worker:

When I entered Baptist College, Springfield, Missouri, I was a typical first-year student, searching for answers to questions. I was not settled on what I was going to do.

During that year something happened that was to change my life. I asked for a Sunday school class at the High Street Baptist Church and was given a little area with a curtain around it, a class book, and one eleven-year-old boy.

I taught this boy for three or four weeks, until he finally brought a friend. I got so discouraged I went to the superintendent with the intention of giving up the class. He told me, "I didn't want to give you the class when you asked because my better judgment told me you were not serious and dedicated. I don't think you will make it in the ministry, but I went against my judgment and gave you the class." The middle-aged man finished, "I was right in my first judgment—you're worthless, so give me the book."

This made me so mad, I told him I would not give him the book and I'd consider the class and pray about it. I went back to my room at the dormitory and began praying. I asked the Dean of Students for a key to an empty room on the third floor, and each afternoon for a week I went and prayed from half-past-one until five o'clock. God broke my heart over my failure with the small Sunday school class.

I realized if I wasn't going to be faithful in little things, God would never bless me in big things. I prayed for the first boy and his family, and the boy he had brought and his family. Next I prayed for myself and my own needs, asking God to lead me to the right place.

God blessed the class, and new kids came. I prayed for them and their friends. On Saturday I cut a swath across every playground and empty lot I could find, seeking eleven-year-old boys. When I left school in May of that year the Lord had given me fifty-six eleven-year-old boys for my class. All had been saved and many of their mothers, dads, and friends had also been saved.[5]

## Becoming Self-Motivated

Self-motivation is a quality that can be adopted from great achievers and developed in your own life. Frequently referred to as the Michelangelo of the twentieth century, Pablo Picasso drove himself mercilessly toward perfection. Beyond his personal accomplishments, Picasso's professional accomplishments are inconceivable. Think of a man producing two hundred thousand pieces of art in seventy-five years![6]

Self-motivation emerges when you are centered in your purpose. Failure, at times, may be the result of your operating outside of your calling and purpose. The principles you glean from other achievers should not cause you to forget your own life's purpose. Each of us has a set purpose ordained by our Creator. Each of us must labor to determine and discern our life's calling. Whatever that may be, it will be the place where we ultimately find success. Success is not based on fame, money, or power. It comes when you fulfill the very purpose for which you were created.

148

During the early phase of my engineering career, I was in the center of God's will for that period of my life. As a result, I experienced feelings of joy, peace, and inner satisfaction. However, once God called me out of that field, the peace and joy I had known previously began to wane, reflecting that the will of God had shifted, as it related to my vocations. When God called me out, I did not move in His timing. Out of fear and apprehension, I lingered at the consulting firm until the pressure of disobedience weighed too heavily on my heart. My wife and I finally agreed to trust God financially, and I resigned from the engineering field. We had begun pioneering a church approximately two years prior to this time, and it was still small. But in obedience to the will of God, I submitted myself to His leadership. Today, the fruit of my obedience is known on an international level. I am working in the field to which He has called me. I am doing the will of God for my life.

Self-motivation flourishes when you begin to appreciate the job you have, the family you've been blessed with, and the uniqueness of God's tender workings in your life. You can easily form the right perspective of life when you take a look at someone who is not as fortunate as you are. A man stops complaining about the shoes that don't fit him when he meets a man who has no feet. Perspective is a good motivator. You need both the achievers and underachievers around you to bring your life into a healthy balance. Underachievers help you learn to help others and appreciate what you have. Achievers push you beyond their successes so that, eventually, you can learn to push yourself.

*Carpe diem.* Seize the day! Ask God to bring the right coach into your life. Then work hard and motivate yourself to reach your goals.

## —— Chapter 9 ——

# YOU LOOK FUNNY!

*A cheerful heart is good medicine, but a crushed*
*spirit dries up the bones.*
—*Proverbs 17:22*

I walked into the barbershop one morning hoping to find it empty so that I wouldn't have to wait long. For the past week or so, I had been putting off this much-needed haircut because the lines are usually so long. But as soon as I walked into the shop I became discouraged. The place was filled with waiting patrons. There were three or four barbers working busily; I didn't recognize one of them, but it didn't matter because I was waiting for my usual barber.

In a few minutes the new barber's chair became available. "Next," he yelled. No one moved. Then he pointed about ten feet to the left of me and said, "You're next!" No one moved. He became irritated and kept pointing about ten feet from me and shouted, "Can't you hear me? You're next!"

Since no one else spoke up, I said, "Who, me?"

"Yeah, you," he said. "Can't you see I've been talking to you? You're next in line."

When I looked directly at him, I realized why he was pointing ten feet away from me. The barber was cross-eyed. "C'mon, hurry up," he said. "There are other people waiting. You're next."

Although I felt pressured to sit in his chair, I was worried about what kind of haircut I would receive—especially since he couldn't even point to the spot where I was sitting! Reluctantly, I got up and went to his chair.

When the man was finished, there were dips and craters in my hair. Not only that! My hair was slanted upward on one side. I looked like that cartoon character Gumby! I looked comical—no, ridiculous! There was nothing I could do. I would have to live with this look until my hair grew back in. I was so angry. What would I say to people? How would I live with this look? Somehow, I had to learn to cope with this mistake.

## LEARNING TO LAUGH AT YOURSELF

Gaining the ability to laugh at oneself is a major milestone in life. Although we are afforded plenty of opportunities to chuckle at our own silly mistakes, we seldom use them. These personal comical moments can be therapeutic and stress relieving if we learn the value they bring. A failure is a person who has blundered and is not able to cash in on the experience. True success is the ability to enjoy life—every aspect of life. One of the best skills a person can have is the ability to find humor in the midst of pain. A mistake is proof that at least you were trying to accomplish something! My haircut caused a lot of pain, yet I came to the point where I was able to laugh at myself every time I passed a mirror. Jokingly I would say to myself, "You look like Gumby."

Now, something as light and frivolous as a haircut doesn't compare with the weight of a major failure. Yet the principles to be learned are applicable to virtually every awkward situation in life. To have potential moments of healing at your fingertips but not take advantage of them is another mistake. It would be wonderful if mistakes could be sold for as much as they cost us. Since there is no market for them, you should learn to benefit from their inherent value.

## WHO ARE YOU TRYING TO IMPRESS?

We each have a choice as to how we'll respond in a crisis, particularly a crisis of our own doing. Laugh or cry—it's up to you. There is no right or wrong—no moral absolute, no biblical norm that you're to follow when it comes to the subject of laughter. The only absolute you must adhere to is to not sin against God or other people. In the aftermath of a crisis, many people attempt to hide their anger toward God and other people. But in order to achieve healing, a number of remedies can help, such as times of introspection, prayer, and perhaps counseling. Once God deals with your heart on the issue of personal honesty, the matter is resolved. Your anger toward Him is abated. You are back to normal. But it's far more difficult to learn to laugh at your failures.

One Saturday afternoon when I was home alone, I decided to wash the lunch dishes. After loading the dishwasher, I realized that we didn't have any dishwashing detergent. So I decided to pour a little regular dishwashing liquid into the dishwasher. After all, I thought, dishwashing liquid is made of the same ingredients as dishwasher detergent. In a few moments, I learned otherwise. After I turned on the dishwasher, I left the room to watch television. In about ten minutes, I returned to the kitchen to find soapsuds all over the floor. They had leaked out of the dishwasher and were still coming out rapidly.

I knew that my family would be returning shortly from their shopping trip. I began to work feverishly to clean the floor so that they wouldn't find out I had done something foolish. I was trying to spare myself an embarrassing moment. But the more I wiped the floor, the more the soapsuds leaked out of the machine. I felt like a character on one of those zany sitcoms. Finally, after about fifteen minutes of playing catch-up with the dishwasher, the floor was all mopped and clean, though I had never anticipated cleaning the floor.

The moment I finished wiping the floor, my wife and daughters walked into the house. The first place they went was the kitchen. The minute I had heard the garage door open, I had run to the family room to watch television. I wanted to be as far away from the scene of the crime as possible. As they walked through the kitchen and into the family room, my wife said, "Oh, I see that you washed the dishes."

"Yes, honey," I said. "I wanted to surprise everyone."

My youngest, Jessica, asked, "Daddy, how come you're sweating so much?"

I hadn't thought about wiping my brow. Because I was so concerned about saving face, the thought of sweat dripping from me didn't enter my mind. I said, "Honey, it's nothing at all."

Then my older daughter began to press the issue further, thinking that something about Dad's statement smelled fishy. As Danielle pressed more and more, I finally gave in and told them the whole story. They laughed and laughed and laughed at my blunder. My wife, Marlinda, joined in, saying, "Didn't you know that you can't put dishwashing liquid into the dishwasher?"

In frustration, I said, "I do now!" But to heal my bruised ego, I began laughing at my blunder.

Who was I trying to impress? My family? The people who love me? It wasn't necessary. One faux pas wasn't going to shatter my image in their eyes. Saving face is something that people try their hardest to do. Yet the highest form of self-respect is to admit mistakes and make amends for them. En route to making corrections there should be a little chuckle. This shows that you've learned to not take yourself too seriously. Failure has a way of making you buckle down and grit your teeth at life. "I'll never let this happen again!" you declare. "How could I have been so senseless?" As you say this, you're vowing to walk through life in a hard-nosed, more serious way. These kinds of resolutions have a way of making you tougher, but less enjoyable to be around.

True success in life is not to make all the people around you impressed with your achievements and impeccable track record. Rather, true success is when people like you regardless of where you go and when you get there. Granted, life is complicated, and many painful, unexplainable tragedies befall us. Bank balances can never measure success. Money only measures financial stability. Success is a matter of character. A person who has achieved success never has to prove it. The reason why big spenders throw their money and credentials around is that they are trying to prove to others—and to themselves—that they are successful. Success involves the willingness to be reckoned a failure in everyone's eyes except God's.

Real success means that you've learned that true value is in enjoying life. This means that you know how to relax. You no longer allow the opinions of others to shape your opinion of yourself. Enjoying life is knowing how to have a candlelight dinner when you're unable to pay your light bill, or fasting when you have no food in the refrigerator. No one can make up your mind to have the right attitude but you. Decide today not to live to please people, but to please God. Have a good time with your life. Enjoy laughing at your blunders. Discover a new and winning attitude for life, in the spirit of Henry Wadsworth Longfellow, who wrote:

Not in the clamor of the crowded street,
Not in the shouts and plaudits of the throng,
But in ourselves are triumph and defeat.[1]

## A Cheerful Heart Is Good Medicine

In Solomon's desire to perpetuate the success of the human race, he penned a thought that cannot be ignored if you are to obtain victory over life's mishaps. He wrote, "*A cheerful heart is good medicine, but a crushed spirit dries up the bones*" (Proverbs 17:22). Whenever you hear laughter, does the thought of medicine or healing ever come to mind? Prior to my reading and studying this portion of Scripture, I had a vague understanding of the therapeutic nature of laughter. Though I had experienced this type of healing when I took time to socialize with friends, I never really understood how and why laughter works in such a medicinal way.

If laughter and merrymaking were not essential parts of life, God would not have created them. Just imagine how the world would be if laughter were removed. If one solitary chuckle could no longer be found, what would the impact be on families, marriages, jobs, and so forth? Stand-up comedy is a multibillion dollar industry. And it's not going anywhere because it fills a societal need. Every day all kinds of situation comedies are aired on television to entertain viewers.

The zany comedy *Seinfeld*, featuring Jerry Seinfeld, became so popular in the late 1990s that tens of millions tuned in each night to see the antics of Jerry and his three friends. The show became so successful that Jerry Seinfeld was earning $1 million for each thirty-minute episode. That's a whole lot of money just to make people laugh about ridiculous, nonessential things. The millions Seinfeld earned didn't turn viewers or sponsors away. Rather, his ingenuity kept people watching each week.

## LAUGHTER IS HEALING

To have a merry heart is to possess something deeper than the laughter that takes place at a social gathering. A merry heart is evidence that one has the right focus on life. It also reflects the reality that although everything may not be perfect, relaxation from worry is necessary to obtain victory over unusual circumstances. A merry heart communicates the reality that "down time"—time of reflection—is just as important as hard work. Hard work speaks of focused energy directed at achieving, conquering, or overcoming obstacles. Down time is not synonymous with idle time. Rather, it is a response to listening to one's heart and conscience, which tells you that you've been running too much. A merry heart is a reflective heart. It's a heart that rehearses past actions in order to avoid making the same mistakes again. A merry heart is one that realizes that life should be enjoyed and not just lived. Down time is needed to restore your energy and rejuvenate your soul.

One man challenged another to an all-day wood-chopping contest. The challenger worked very hard, stopping only for a brief lunch break. The other man had a leisurely lunch and took several breaks during the day. At the end of the day, the challenger was surprised and annoyed to find that the other fellow had chopped substantially more wood than he had.

"I don't get it," he said. "Every time I checked, you were taking a rest, yet you chopped more wood than I did."

"But you didn't notice," said the winning woodsman, "that when I sat down to rest, I was sharpening my ax."

A merry heart sharpens the ax of one's life. Your dreams, ambitions, and purposes can be accomplished more readily because of the healing that a merry heart provides. The deception that "all work and no play" will help you to arrive at your destination more quickly is just that—a deception. Activity and accomplishment are two entirely different things. Life must be lived in such a way that time is scheduled just to laugh at life and at oneself. Down time must be guarded just as carefully as work time. Accomplishments take place because the internal engine has been recharged through laughter and fun. If you can't laugh at yourself, you'll find yourself in a constant depression, sulking over your defeats and failures. The deception of this kind of depression is that more activity, piled high and wide, will help you reach your destination faster. Actually, just the opposite is the truth. This is why the woodsman who took frequent breaks to rejuvenate himself and to sharpen his ax won the contest! Activity is not synonymous with accomplishment.

John Henry Fabre, the great French naturalist, conducted a most unusual experiment with processionary caterpillars—caterpillars that will blindly follow a caterpillar in front of them. Fabre carefully arranged these caterpillars around the rim of a flowerpot, so that the lead caterpillar actually touched the last one, making a complete circle. In the center of the flowerpot he put pine needles, which is the food of the processionary caterpillar. The caterpillars started around the circular flowerpot.

Around and around they went, hour after hour, day after day, night after night. For seven full days and nights, they went around the flowerpot. Finally, they dropped dead of starvation and exhaustion. With an abundance of food less than six inches away, they literally starved to death—all because they confused activity with accomplishment.

Many people make the same mistake. As a result, they reap only a small fraction of the harvest life has to offer. Despite the fact that untold prosperity lies within their reach, they acquire very little of it because they blindly follow the crowd, in a circle leading nowhere. They follow methods and procedures for no reason other than "It's always been done that way." They stay busy performing more and more activities rather than doing the things that yield accomplishments. But a merry heart might provide them with the leisure they need away from their trials, in order to rejuvenate their spirits.

Scientists who have studied the effect of laughter on human beings have found that laughter has a profound and instantaneous effect on virtually every important organ in the human body. Laughter reduces health-sapping tensions and relaxes the tissues, as well as exercising the vital organs. It's said that laughter, even when forced, results in beneficial effects on both the mind and the body. The next time you feel nervous and jittery, indulge in a good laugh. Laughter is a tranquilizer with no side effects.

## A CRUSHED SPIRIT DRIES UP THE BONES

Further examination of Solomon's proverb, *"A cheerful heart is good medicine, but a crushed spirit dries up the bones,"* reveals another insight that can help you combat the repercussions failure can bring. The latter part of this verse indicates that a crushed (depressed or dejected) spirit occurs in the absence of cheerfulness. The result of such depression is dried-up bones. In the Hebrew language and culture, bones represented the body. "Dry" bones signified unhealthiness and lifelessness (cf., Ezekiel 37:1–4); "fat" bones signified a healthy body (Proverbs 3:8; 15:30; 16:24). Thus, your outlook on life can either enhance or destroy your quality of health. Good health is one of the dividends that a cheerful heart pays.

## HEALTHY OUTLOOK, HEALTHY BODY

Your psychological condition affects your physical condition. Sorrow of the soul and sickness of the body are related. Failure is often accompanied by depression and deep sorrow of the soul. God's healing power can in fact be thwarted when a sick person refuses to be cheered up, choosing instead to submerge himself in feelings of loneliness, bitterness, and discouragement. The Reverend W. Harris makes these insightful observations: "A physician always tries to keep his patient in good spirits, and when he discerns that he is weighed down by some mental burden, he wisely seeks to lighten that as well as administer remedies to the body. And when a man is in health cheerfulness of disposition tends to keep him so; while a depressed condition of mind makes him a more easy prey to disease."[2]

Granted, we still lack understanding of the relationship between the emotional well-being of the soul and the health of the body. However, we can see the reality of this mutual dependency and the benefit of having a cheerful outlook on life. Consider the times when you were sick. Did it matter whether your perspective was positive or negative? What effect did your decision to simply relax and stop fighting the reality of your situation have on you? I have found that when my thoughts were positive and my outlook cheerful, I felt better physically. When I was gloomy and felt sorry for myself, the sickness dragged on.

A cheerful heart combats discouragement and disillusionment by offering new assurances. A brighter outlook helps to build a new foundation of confidence and joy. At first the notion of a connection between cheerfulness and healing may sound utterly ridiculous. Yet throughout history, when medical science was not as advanced as it is today, a primary function of the medical community was to improve the spirits of people in distress. A cheerful heart combats sickness and disease because joy is a powerful medicine. Best of all, this medicine is free because you're the manufacturer of it.

The story is told of a young man who came to a renowned doctor in Paris, complaining of depression. He asked the doctor what he could do to get well. The doctor thought of a lighthearted young man named Grimaldi, a leader of café society, who cut a wide swath through the Paris nightlife. The doctor told the young man, "Introduce yourself to Grimaldi. Let him show you how to enjoy yourself, and you will get well."

The downcast young patient looked up with a cynical smile and said, "I am Grimaldi."[3]

The moral of the story is that happiness is not to be found in the fleeting moments of high society living or in the laughter of the dance clubs. Rather, a merry heart is the result a person gains by determining not to allow gloom and disappointment to rule over his soul. This person uses his faith in God to grasp the strength to smile and hope for a better tomorrow. To achieve this state, a person must want to intentionally bear the fruit of joy. Developing such a quality is a deliberate act—a conscious effort to avoid the pitfalls that failure brings. Cheerfulness is not an event. It is not based on what happens or does not happen to you. It is a volitional choice to smile when the facts are telling you to weep.

In the years preceeding World War II, a group of Christian nurses in the Ellen Mitchell Memorial Hospital in Moulmein, Burma, discussed this question during their Tuesday morning Bible hour: "What does it take to make a Christian?" They agreed that true repentance and acceptance of forgiveness placed one in the Christian fold.

Then they asked what it took to build an ever stronger Christian personality. They listed more than twenty-five characteristics that are needed. Faith was placed first on the list, followed by service and love. Dr. Martha Gifford, who reported this experience in a letter to the Woman's American Baptist Foreign Mission Society, wrote:

Some were convinced that cheerfulness must surely be a part of a Christian personality, especially of those who work among the suffering. Who ever knew a grumpy old grouch who "cranks" all the time helping a sick person to get well? It is the "merry heart [that] doeth good like a medicine," and we decided that no matter what the circumstances, a smile three times a day and at bedtime should be a minimum in a Christian hospital.[4]

A healthy outlook does affect your health. Find ways to cheer yourself up. Situations improve when your emotional perspective improves. They are dependent on one another. Your healing lies within the reservoir of joy God has placed deep within your heart.

### SOME THINGS ARE JUST BEYOND YOUR CONTROL

A big dog saw a little dog chasing its tail and asked, "Why are you chasing your tail so?"

Said the puppy, "I have mastered philosophy; I have solved the problems of the universe which no dog before me has rightly solved; I have learned that the best thing for a dog is happiness, and that happiness is my tail. Therefore I am chasing it; and when I catch it, I shall have happiness."

Said the old dog, "My son, I, too, have paid attention to the problems of the universe in my weak way, and I have formed some opinions. I, too, have judged that happiness is a fine thing for a dog, and that happiness is in my tail. But I have noticed that when I chase after it, it keeps running away from me, but when I go about my business, it comes after me."[5]

Happiness is never found by chasing after something, tangible or intangible. Nor will you find it in a human relationship, no matter how kind and gentle your friend may be. There is never a perfect relationship or a relationship that can fulfill all of your dreams every second of your life. There is a higher value from which joy stems. It is walking with God and choosing to be content in every predicament life throws your way. To achieve this kind of contentment is a major feat. Although it may sound farfetched or theoretical, it can be attained. And once you've developed this inner resolve, you will no longer be defeated when everything doesn't go as planned.

Plans, goals, and desires, no matter how noble, are elusive. They can evaporate right before your eyes. Yet if you decide—as the apostle Paul did—to be content in everything, you can peacefully get through any failure. True victory is not when you achieve all of your goals and overcome all of your obstacles; it's when you master your attitude and perspective. Paul wrote:

> *[11]Not that I was ever in need, for I have learned how to get along happily whether I have much or little. [12]I know how to live on almost nothing or with everything. I have learned the secret of contentment in every situation, whether it be a full stomach or hunger, plenty or want; [13]for I can do everything God asks me to with the help of Christ who gives me the strength and power.*
>
> —(Philippians 4:11–13 TLB)

Despite Paul's pedigree—a Hebrew of the Hebrews, a student of Gamaliel, a leading teacher in Jerusalem—when he wrote this passage, he was in prison for his faith. Tradition indicates that prior to his Christian conversion, Paul was an influential member of the Sanhedrin, the most significant Jewish governing body. Yet his status and position in Jewish society had dropped significantly following his conversion. The Jewish community rejected and disowned him as an outcast. As Paul matured in his apostolic calling, he became a humble servant of the gospel and the church. From a prison cell, Paul was able to introduce this positive perspective on life to the Philippian Christians because his focus was not limited to his earthly accomplishments. His goal was to instruct the burgeoning church in how they, too, could experience continuous peace and joy in spite of life's difficulties. Paul's directive to the church was that they draw their strength from their spiritual intimacy with Christ, as he had learned to do.

Often a person's biggest weakness can become his greatest strength. Take, for example, the story of a ten-year-old boy who decided to study judo despite the fact that he had lost his left arm in a devastating car accident. The boy began lessons with an old Japanese judo master. After three months of training, the boy was doing well, but he couldn't understand why the master had taught him only one move.

"Sensei," the boy finally said, "shouldn't I be learning more moves?"

"This is the only move you know, but this is the only move you'll ever need to know," the sensei replied. Not quite understanding but believing his teacher, the boy kept training.

Several months later, the sensei took the boy to his first tournament. Surprising himself, the boy easily won his first two matches. The third match proved to be more difficult, but after some time, his opponent became impatient and charged; the boy deftly used his one move to win the match. Still amazed by his success, the boy was now in the finals. This time, his opponent was bigger, stronger, and more experienced. For a while, the boy appeared to be overmatched. Concerned that the boy might get hurt, the referee called a time-out. He was about to end the match when the sensei intervened.

"No," the sensei insisted, "let him continue."

Soon after the match resumed, the boy's opponent made a critical mistake: He dropped his guard. Instantly, the boy used his move to pin him. He had won the match and the tournament. He was the champion! On the way home, the boy and the sensei reviewed each move in each and every match. Then the boy summoned the courage to ask what was really on his mind.

"Sensei, how did I win the tournament with only one move?"

"You won for two reasons," the sensei answered. "First, you've almost mastered one of the most difficult throws in all of judo. And second, the only known defense for that move is for your opponent to grab your left arm."[6]

The boy's biggest weakness had become his greatest strength. Champions are made because they choose to walk the high road. Though this road may appear more challenging, it offers great rewards. Your perspective of your failure can make or break you. Decide right now that you will not allow this temporary state of affairs to cripple your prospects for a healthy future. Make a determined effort to become *better* not *bitter.* The Bible says, "*Weeping may remain for a night, but rejoicing comes in the morning*" (Psalm 30:5). Guess what? It's morning! Open up the tightly drawn shades of your life and breathe in a fresh new outlook on the victorious days that lie ahead. Make a happy exit from the valley of failure, and adopt a positive perspective as you move toward recovery.

Choosing to not allow discouragement to crush your spirit will yield great fruit. Like the boy with one arm who learned only one move, you must learn to laugh at yourself because it is your only defense against the discouragement that failure brings. Take a moment and laugh right now! Laugh at how complex everything in your life has become. Laugh at the paradox of your situation. Laugh because two years ago you could never have imagined that you'd be in the pickle you're presently in. You owe it to yourself; use your one move. Laugh.

# Chapter 10

# CAN YOU HANDLE SUCCESS?

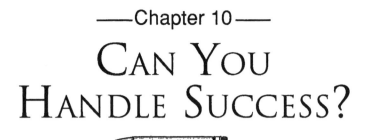

*Success is to be measured not so much by the*
*position that one has reached*
*in life, as by the obstacles that one has*
*overcome while trying to succeed.*
*—Booker T. Washington*

Afr actor/director Michael Douglas had starred in five block-buster films, his father, actor Kirk Douglas, wrote him a note. It said, "Michael, I'm more proud of how you handle success than I am of your success." It's a note Michael Douglas treasures.[1]

If you were to accomplish everything that's in your heart to do, would you be able to handle your success? This is a question that must be regularly asked and answered along the road to achieving your destiny. The question forces you to become introspective. It causes you to probe deep within to determine whether your values are being compromised in any way. The other question you cannot avoid is "What makes me a success?" Everyone has his own definition of success. Yet if you apply someone else's definition to your life, it may be inappropriate. The result may cause more harm than good. Whether the other person's definition is too overwhelming because it's so far above you or too insulting because it's far beneath you, another's definition of success will always be wrong for you.

You must labor to come up with a comfortable meaning of the word success so that your goals will not be emotionally damaging to you. I've known many people who've lived within the definitions others have imposed upon them. As a consequence, they applied to schools and studied subjects they were not gifted in, worked in fields they did not enjoy, and married people they did not want to marry. All these things were done just to please the people they considered significant in their lives. But the blame cannot be placed on anyone other than the ones who lacked the courage to break out of the limitations placed on them by others.

I've come across at least a hundred definitions of success while writing this book. Some are funny, some witty, and others quite motivational to someone who is struggling with failure. Most of them are very good. I'll share only a few with you, specifically the ones that I feel capture the heart of God and my purpose in writing this book.

> Success is in the way you walk the paths of life each day;
> it's in the little things you do, and in the things you say.
> Success is not in getting rich, or rising high to fame.
> It's not alone in winning goals, which all men hope to
> claim. Success is being big of heart, and clean and broad
> in mind; it's being faithful to your friends, and to the
> stranger, kind. It's in the children whom you love, and all
> they learn from you; success depends on character, and
> everything you do.[2]

The basic rules for success may be defined as follows: Know what you want. Find out what it takes to get it. Act on it and persevere.[3]

Success is an individual determination based on what each of us deems to be a worthwhile goal. A rewarding objective gives you personal pleasure in planning and dreaming about the future. It satisfies the reason behind the hard work and gives you impetus to reject the rejections. It motivates you to go beyond your own resources and recruit encouragers, mentors, and personal life-management specialists to assist you in accomplishing your dream. To achieve success, you must not procrastinate or sulk about because of your failure. The key to achieving victory is to start from where you are and to map out an action plan that can carry you beyond the present state of mediocrity into the winner's circle.

## START WHERE YOU ARE

A driver pulled over to the side of the road one evening and asked a pedestrian how he could get to Grove Street. The pedestrian stopped and looked around. Then he said, "If you go down one block and turn right—oops, you can't go that way. The street is under construction. Well, go north for two blocks and turn left. Nah, that won't work either. It's a one-way street."

The pedestrian scratched his head as he thought about what to say next. Then he said, "Turn around and go two blocks and make a left. Well, there's water damage on that road; you can't go that way." In frustration, the pedestrian finally said to the driver, "You shouldn't be lost here! You should be lost somewhere else!"

How about that! You should be lost somewhere else. The problem is, when you're lost, you have to start from where you are in forging ahead toward your dream. The way you discover the precise road to your dream is by drawing close to God. This is accomplished through prayer and personal worship. During your prayer time, you should say to the Lord, "God, help me! Lead me out of this whirlwind of confusion I'm feeling. Help me to discern your will for my life and guide me in walking wholeheartedly toward it." You may put the content of this prayer into your own words. The idea, however, is that it's within the context of a close relationship with God that the best action plan will be established. God knows best, and His plan will create the maximum pleasure you could possibly experience.

Jeremiah prophesied God's heart to the Israelites during a period when they were distant from Him because of their sin. He wrote, "'For I know the plans I have for you,' declares the LORD, 'plans to prosper you and not to harm you, plans to give you hope and a future'" (Jeremiah 29:11). This prophecy is applicable to you today. God's will for you is no different than it was for the Israelites in those days. He has plans for your prosperity and future. Therefore, the first step in any action plan should be to draw closer to the Lord.

Second, start from where you are and arise. Arise from the place where failure has tossed you. Establish specific personal goals. Setting goals is a beautiful way to cope with the problems failure brings. Goals create a keen sense of hope. Goals communicate that your life is not over. They restore faith to your life. The act of working toward your goals draws from the energy deep within you, so that your life can progress to a greater point of fulfillment. Goals announce that there are more years ahead of you—brighter, more pleasant years.

An action plan isn't some exercise in futility. It is a well thought-out plan that centers on accomplishing several practical steps. A clever acronym to aid you in formulating your goal is the word "SMART." The "S" stands for specific. The "M" represents the word measurable. "A" means achievable. "R" stands for realistic, and "T" represents timely. Consequently, a simple, practical action plan should be specific, measurable, achievable, realistic, and timely. If your plan is consistent with these five components, it should be easily implemented. By following this strategy, you'll be taking an aggressive step of faith, saying for all the world to hear, "I have victory over my failure! I'm bigger than my failure!"

Establishing a plan of action is also your acknowledgment of the truthfulness of Scripture. It says that you believe that God's plan concerning you really is to prosper you and give you hope and a future. It's a frontal assault against any demonic power that tries to make you doubt the plan of God. Your plan of action will also help you put feet to your prayers—walking after the known will of God. Arise from your state of affliction and call on the Lord for His wisdom and guidance! Your action plan is a step of courage in the face of all uncertainties and odds. This is the stuff champions are made of. Champions are people of action!

Whatever you do, you'll need courage and faith. Whatever action plan you decide upon, there will always be someone to tell you you're wrong. And there will always be obstacles arising, tempting you to think that your critics are right. Map out a plan anyway, and stick to it. Success doesn't happen by chance. It's achieved through hard work, a good plan of action, and courage against all odds. Seize the opportunity and invoke the presence of God through heartfelt prayer. Decide right now to do something about your situation. Start by changing your mind about your future.

So what are you going to do today? After you put this book down, then what? Where will you go? Whom will you call on? What about prayer? What are you expecting God to do for you? Get an action plan together! List a few goals! Yes, take the time to write them down. Come back to the plan periodically. Draw strength from the Holy Spirit's leading. Let this moment be a landmark for you as you respond to the Holy Spirit's divine nudging. The Holy Spirit wants to move you strategically onto His path of victory. Allow yourself to be moved. Don't resist! Let go. Ease up. Watch God do something powerful for you. He wants to. It's His will.

## *Failures Are Opportunities For Success*

Somerset Maugham wrote a story about a janitor at St. Peter's Church in London. One day a young vicar discovered that the janitor was illiterate, and fired him. Jobless, the man invested his meager savings in a tiny tobacco shop, where he prospered. He then bought another, expanded it, and ended up with a chain of tobacco stores worth several hundred thousand dollars.

One day the man's banker said, "You've done well for an illiterate, but where would you be if you could read and write?"

"Well," replied the man, "I'd be janitor of St. Peter's Church in Neville Square."[4]

## *Don't Compromise Your Personal Integrity*

It has been said that integrity is who you are in the dark, when no one else is looking. The word integrity comes from the word integral. It is a form of another word, integrated. When you're living in integrity, it means that your whole life is integrated. There's nothing that smacks of duplicity or hypocrisy. Who you are on the job is who you are at church. Who you are at church is who you are at home. Integrity is the integration of a life.

When the golf ball was first manufactured, it was made of dozens of rubber bands bound tightly together under an exterior cover. The interconnectedness of the rubber bands represents how your life should be connected. The spiritual, natural, sacred, and secular should intersect with one another. This is the model of an integrated life.

The first golf ball had a smooth external cover. But when a golfer would hit the ball, the smooth cover would not allow it to go very far. The designers decided to remanufacture the ball, this time placing defects—imperfections—all over the ball's surface. Now when a golf ball is struck, it goes the distance. The imperfections in your life will also cause you to go the distance. The presence of problems in your life doesn't automatically signify a breach in your personal integrity. How you handle your problems will make that determination. The key is that you must be honest with the Lord about the areas in which you need His help.

An elderly unmarried minister invited a young minister over for dinner. During the meal, the young minister couldn't help but notice how attractive and shapely the housekeeper was. Over the course of the evening, he started to wonder whether there was more between the elderly minister and his housekeeper than met the eye. Reading the young minister's thoughts, the elderly minister volunteered, "I know what you must be thinking, but I assure you, my relationship with my housekeeper is purely professional."

About a week later the housekeeper came to the elderly minister and said, "Reverend, ever since the young minister came to dinner, I've been unable to find the beautiful silver gravy ladle. You don't suppose he took it, do you?"

The minister said, "Well, I doubt it, but I'll write him a letter just to be sure." So he sat down and wrote: "Dear Reverend, I'm not saying that you did take the gravy ladle from my house, and I'm not saying you did not take the gravy ladle. But the fact remains that it has been missing ever since you were here."

Several days later the elderly minister received a letter from the young minister which read: "Dear Reverend, I'm not saying that you do sleep with your housekeeper, and I'm not saying that you do not sleep with your housekeeper. But the fact remains that if you were sleeping in your own bed, you would have found the gravy ladle by now."

Maintaining your integrity is a surefire way to know that God is leading you. Be honest about yourself to the Lord. Don't hide or color your actions or thoughts. Integrity will give you peace. There will be a cessation of internal conflict when you decide to walk uprightly before God. Scripture declares, "The man of integrity walks securely, but he who takes crooked paths will be found out" (Proverbs 10:9). Integrity strengthens you in your plans. A secure walk is a walk of stability, strength, and courage. It's a very peaceful feeling to move through life without having to keep looking over your shoulder because you're afraid that someone is going to find you out. Integrity creates a pathway to God's promises. The Bible states, "The integrity of the upright guides them, but the unfaithful are destroyed by their duplicity" (Proverbs 11:3). Integrity moves you closer to your dreams, your goals, and your lifelong objectives.

If there is a breech in your integrity, even a slight one, the solution is repentance. Repentance means "to turn around." It connotes someone who realizes that he's going in the wrong direction, who immediately turns around and begins going in the opposite way. This is what the Lord desires to see take place in your heart. Inappropriate behaviors and relationships must be corrected. What good is compromising your personal integrity in order to win the world? It's not worth it. Nothing is worth having a heart that is polluted. Repentance is not based on feelings or emotions. It requires that you mentally deduce that your direction is wrong—and that you correct it. Many lives have been ravaged by the consequences of sin. Repentance is the escape hatch. Use it! Run to it!

Failure can have a domino effect if your integrity is not upheld. Integrity is the brake that stops the downward trend. When Leonardo da Vinci was painting his masterpiece, "The Last Supper," he selected as the person to pose for his rendering of Christ a young man, Pietri Bandinelli, who was a choirboy at the Milan Cathedral. Many years passed before the great picture was completed, and when one character only—that of Judas Iscariot—remained to be painted, the great artist noticed a man in the streets of Rome. With shoulders bent toward the ground and a cold, hard, even saturnine expression, the man perfectly suited the artist's conception of Judas. Back in the painter's studio, this man began to look around, as if recalling an incident of years gone by. Finally, with a sad look of surprise, he said, "Maestro, I was in this studio twenty-five years ago. I, then, sat for Christ."[5]

Once a person has experienced failure, he becomes vulnerable to all kinds of failures. Quite obviously, all failures are not of a moral nature and may not necessarily have an association with unrighteous behavior. When your moral choices reflect disobedience to God's laws, then heartfelt repentance should occur. Repentance is an acknowledgement of the fact that God is right about His perspective of your sins. Repentance shows that you agree with God's attitude toward your sin. Repentance enables you to have a fresh start. What would you do with a second chance? Here's some good news: God gives second chances. He is the Lord of the second chance. Repentance is the door to the second chance. Even if you've tried to walk through that door before, try again! Failure is written in pencil. It can easily be erased by the Lord.

Repentance is heaven's big eraser, which wipes out your errors. Right now, exercise your integrity. If you know in your heart that your failure has caused you to breach your integrity, fall on your face before God. Your second chance has begun! You are a recipient of the grace of God.

## Loving People, Not Just Projects

What makes a truly successful person is not intelligence, education, life-style, or pedigree. The key factor that determines a person's success is his or her ability to deal gracefully with people. Since failure has a way of bringing you to a greater place of sobriety about the true value and meaning of life, you should plan on spending a lot of time building meaningful relationships. It takes time to build great families and friendships. But because we are sometimes so driven to succeed vocationally, our relationships with friends and family members are often lacking.

One night a wife found her husband standing over their baby's crib. Lately, he had been spending so many hours at work that he had not taken the opportunity to spend time with their new baby. Silently she watched him. As he stood looking down at the sleeping infant, she saw on his face a mixture of emotions—disbelief, doubt, delight, amazement, enchantment, even skepticism.

Touched by this unusual display and with eyes glistening, she slipped her arm around her husband. "A penny for your thoughts," she said.

"It's amazing!" he replied. "I just can't see how anybody can make a crib like that for only $46.50!"

Being away from the people who mean the most to you may cause you to devalue these relationships. For example, a family that had not been spending much time together decided to go to the movies. On the way into the theater, the young son stopped by the refreshment stand to buy popcorn. By the time he got into the theater, the lights were already dim. He scanned the theater and couldn't find his family. He paced up and down the aisles, searching the crowd in the near-darkness. Then, as the lights began to go out completely, he stopped and asked out loud, "Does anyone recognize me?"

The dogged pursuit of your career must not take place at the expense of your family and friendships. Labor to build true friendships—ones that display brotherly affection and love. Just as you desire success in your vocational pursuits, you should cultivate lasting relationships by spending time with friends and family members. If you're not careful, your commitment to projects could corrupt your commitment to the people with whom God has called you to walk. People are important to God. Consequently, fellowship with people must be viewed from that perspective. In fact, the human race is God's most precious creation. If communion with mankind is of the utmost importance to the Creator of the universe, communion with your friends and family should be a high priority as you pursue your destiny.

## WANTED: PEOPLE LOOKING FOR A GREAT CAREER

Some ministers put people to sleep when they preach. Pastor Smith was such a person. Whenever he preached, people in his congregation fell asleep. One Sunday afternoon, discouraged by the number of parishioners who had dozed off during his sermon, Pastor Smith decided that he was going to put an end to all of this. He was going to do something drastic, but it was sure to work. He went to the hardware store and purchased a few long poles with round knobs on the ends. He smiled to himself as he thought about his masterful plan.

The following Sunday, he arrived at the church early to fill the ushers in on his scheme. Each usher was given a long pole and was instructed that if anyone fell asleep, the usher was to hit him on the head and wake him up.

About fifteen minutes into Pastor Smith's sermon, one of the new ushers saw a gentleman dozing off in the pew. He took the pole as instructed, reached across the congregation, and hit the man on the head. The man suddenly collapsed right on the floor! Apparently, the eager usher had hit the man too hard and he passed out.

There was a lot of commotion as people gathered around the unconscious man. The usher forced his way through the crowd to see what he could do. Wisely, he pulled out some smelling salts and passed them under the nose of the man. Slowly, the injured man began to regain his composure. But as he was becoming alert, he said to the usher, "I can still hear the pastor's voice! Hit me again!"

If you focus your attention only on the task at hand, rather than on connecting with people, you may find yourself in the same boat as Pastor Smith. He labored at the task of preaching, but he did so as if in a vacuum. He didn't realize that his audience had turned him off because he had not connected with them. Don't sacrifice the people in your life in order to succeed in the pursuit of projects. True success is the ability to pour yourself into the lives of those around you while accomplishing your personal goals. Make your connection with people, not only with tasks.

## INCLUDE GOD IN EVERY AREA OF YOUR LIFE

Success can also be defined as the complete alignment of your life with the will of God. It's the ability to see your faults and shortcomings through the eyes of God's grace. The apostle Paul struggled with feelings of weakness, thinking he lacked the strength to accomplish what was in his heart. Out of his personal pleadings with God came one of the most moving passages of sacred Scripture:

> *[7]To keep me from becoming conceited because of these surpassingly great revelations, there was given me a thorn in my flesh, a messenger of Satan, to torment me. [8]Three times I pleaded with the Lord to take it away from me. [9]But he said to me, "My grace is sufficient for you, for my power is made perfect in weakness." Therefore I will boast all the more gladly about my weaknesses, so that Christ's power may rest on me.*
> *[10]That is why, for Christ's sake, I delight in weaknesses, in insults, in hardships, in persecutions, in difficulties. For when I am weak, then I am strong.*
>
> —(2 Corinthians 12:7–10)

Paul realized that his weaknesses were opportunities for God's grace to take center stage. This realization changed his paradigm. He no longer saw hardships and difficulties as failures. Rather, these weaknesses could be used to draw Paul closer to Christ. They proved to keep him dependent on God. Paul experienced an amazing victory over his circumstances through this change in perspective. His life would never be the same again. He could laugh at his situation, no matter how perplexing it may have been. Paul realized that his personal worth was not based on what he did, what he had, or whom he was with. It was based solely on who he was as a person. His weaknesses, when viewed through the lens of God's grace, gave the Lord an opportunity to display His wonderful power.

Although the apostle may not have done everything right, God did not lessen His display of grace on his behalf. In fact, Paul became aware that God wanted to include Himself in every area of his life— even his weaknesses. Likewise, your personal shortcomings won't hinder God. God inhabits our past, present, and future weaknesses.

A boy entered a pet store and asked the owner how much a puppy cost. "From thirty to fifty dollars," the owner replied.

Reaching into his pocket, the boy pulled out several coins. "I have $2.37," he said. "May I please see them?"

The proprietor smiled and whistled. Out of a kennel came Lady, followed by five tiny, adorable puppies. One puppy, however, was lagging behind the others. Immediately, the boy's attention was on the slower, limping puppy. "What's wrong with that one?" he asked.

The owner explained that his veterinarian had discovered that the puppy was missing a hip socket. "He will always be lame and walk with a limp," he added.

The little boy became very excited and said, "I'll take that one!"

"Nah," the owner argued. "I couldn't sell you that one. He's flawed. If you really want him, I'll just give him to you."

The little boy became angry, looked the man in the eye, and said, "I don't want you to give him to me. This puppy is worth just as much as these other puppies. I'll pay full price. I'll give you $2.37 now and fifty cents a month until I've paid for him."

"But young man," the owner persisted, "you really don't want this puppy. He won't be able to run and jump and play with you like the others could."

The young boy reached down and rolled up his pant leg, revealing a badly twisted left leg, supported by a metal brace. He looked up at the store owner and softly said, "Well, I don't run so well myself, and this little puppy will need someone who understands."[6]

In God's infinite wisdom, He sent Christ into the world to identify with our weaknesses and failures. Jesus suffered loss, pain, rejection, discouragement, and attacks from people who thought they were better than He was. Yet He died for the sins of the world without questioning or wavering in His mission. Mark captured Jesus' heart for people who have experienced failure when he recorded the Lord's words: "People who are well do not need a doctor, but only those who are sick. I have not come to call the respectable people, but the outcasts" (Mark 2:17 TEV). If you've experienced failure in your life, congratulations! You're the kind of person whom Jesus is calling to stand by His side. Even if you walk with a limp, walking with Jesus makes you a winner. Like the little boy who paid full price for the crippled puppy, Jesus paid full price for you. You're valuable to God despite what you've been through. After all, He's the originator of the phrase: Failure is written in pencil.

# End Notes

## *Chapter 1: The Spagetti Factory*

1. Harry Verploegh, *The Quotable Tozer* (Camp Hill, Pa.: Christian Publications, 1994), 49.

2. John Bunyan, *Pilgrim's Progress* (Chicago: Moody Press, 1960), 29.

3. James S. Hewitt, ed., *Illustrations Unlimited* (Wheaton: Tyndale House Publishers, 1988), 205.

4. Rob Gilbert, ed., *Bits & Pieces,* (Fairfield, N.J.: The Economics Press). Vol. R, no.5 (1998:13).

## *Chapter 2: The Benefits of Failure*

1. Paul Lee Tan, Electronic Edition: Encyclopedia of 7,700 Illustrations (Rockville, Md.: Assurance Publishers, 1996).

2. The McGraw-Hill Encyclopedia of World Biography (New York: McGraw-Hill Book Company, 1973), 539–43.

3. Christopher Power, res. dir., *The Experts Speak* (New York: Pantheon Books, 1984).

4. Warren Bennis, Richard Mason, and Ian Mitroff, eds., *The Jossey-Bass Management Series* (San Francisco: Jossey-Bass Publisher, 1987), 63.

5. Edmund Fuller, *Thesaurus of Anecdotes* (New York: Crown Publishers, 1942), 196.

6. Gilbert Brim, *Ambition: How We Manage Success and Failure Throughout Our Lives* (New York: BasicBooks, 1992), 111–12.

7. Eusebius Pamphilus, *Ecclesiastical History*, trans. Christian Frederick Cruse (Grand Rapids: Baker Book House, 1981), 65.
8. Williard F. Harley, Jr., and Jennifer Harley Chalmers, *Surviving an Affair* (Grand Rapids: Fleming H. Revell, 1998), 16.
9. *Narcotics Anonymous* (Van Nuys, Calif.: World Service Office, 1988), 26.
10. J. Oswald Chambers, Electronic Edition: Daily Devotional Readings. *My Utmost For His Highest* (Grand Rapids: Discovery House Publishers, 1989).
11. Tan, Electronic Edition: *Encyclopedia of 7,700 Illustrations.*

### Chapter 3: Reject the Rejection

1. Hewitt, *Illustrations Unlimited*, 185.
2. Gilbert, ed., *Bits & Pieces*, Vol. T/No, 10 (1998:2).
3. Ibid., Vol. T/No, 10 (1998:2).
4. *Webster's New World College Dictionary*, 3d ed., s.v. "reject."
5. Hewitt, *Illustrations Unlimited*, 19–20.
6. Gilbert, ed., *Bits & Pieces*, Vol. T/No, 10 (1998:4).
7. Hewitt, *Illustrations Unlimited*, 205.
8. James Montgomery Boice, *Foundations of the Christian Faith* (Downers Grove, Ill.: InterVarsity Press, 1986), 139.
9. Hewitt, *Illustrations Unlimited*, 155.

### Chapter 4: What Are You Holding On To?

1. Charles H. Spurgeon, *The Treasury of David*, vol. 1 (Peabody, Mass.: Hendrickson Publishers), 407.
2. Kenneth S. Wuest, *Word Studies in the Greek New Testament*, vol. 2 (Grand Rapids: Eerdmans Publishing Company, 1973), 217.

3. *Webster's New World College Dictionary*, 3d ed., s.v. "punishment."

4. Spiros Zodhiates, *The Complete Word Study Dictionary: New Testament* (Chattanooga: AMG Publishers, 1993), 874.

## Chapter 5: Bringing Order Out of Chaos

1. Hewitt, Illustrations Unlimited, 122.

2. G. Curtis Jones, 1,000 Illustrations for Preaching and Teaching (Nashville: Broadman Press, 1986), 134.

3. Warren Baker, gen. ed., The Complete Word Study: Old Testament (Chattanooga: AMG Publishers, 1994), 2353.

4. F. W. Krummacher, Elijah the Tishbite (Grand Rapids: Kregel Publications, 1992), 121–22.

5. Hewitt, Illustrations Unlimited, 197.

## Chapter 6: Who Can You Turn To?

1. Tan, Electronic Edition: *Encyclopedia of 7,700 Illustrations*.

2. Ibid.

3. Ibid.

4. Gilbert, ed., *Bits & Pieces*, 16 July 1998, p5.

5. Tan, Electronic Edition: *Encyclopedia of 7,700 Illustrations*.

6. Dennis Rainey and Barbara Rainey, *Building Your Mate's Self-Esteem* (Nashville: Thomas Nelson, 1993), 111.

7. Tan, Electronic Edition: *Encyclopedia of 7,700 Illustrations*.

8. Rob Gilbert, ed., *The Best of Bits & Pieces* (Fairfield, N.J.: The Economics Press, 1994), 60.

9. Gilbert, ed., *Bits & Pieces*, Vol. T/No. 15, p9–11.

### *Chapter 7: He Bit His Ear!*

1. C. S. Lewis, *The Problem of Pain* (New York: Simon & Schuster, 1996), 140.
2. Chambers, Electronic Edition: Daily Devotional Readings. *My Ut most for His Highest.*
3. Ibid.
4. Thomas á Kempis, Electronic Edition: *The Imitation of Christ* (Oak Harbor, Wash.: Logos Research Systems, 1996).
5. Joachim Jeremias, *The Parables of Jesus* (Upper Saddle River, N.J.: Prentice-Hall, 1972), 153.
6. John R. Donahue, *The Gospel in Parable*, (Philadelphia: Fortress Press, 1988), 184.
7. Ibid., 183.
8. Hewitt, *Illustrations Unlimited*, 16.
9. Gilbert, ed., *The Best of Bits & Pieces*, 62–63.
10. Archibald Hunter, *Interpreting the Parables* (Philadelphia: The Westminster Press, 1960), 69.

### *Chapter 8: Okay, Coach!*

1. Hewitt, *Illustrations Unlimited*, 196.
2. Gilbert, ed., *Bits & Pieces*, (Fairfield, N.J.: The Economics Press) 16 July 1998, p. 16-17
3. Bobb Biehl, *Mentoring* (Nashville: Broadman & Holman Publishers, 1996), 13.
4. Paul D. Stanley and J. Robert Clinton, *Connecting* (Colorado Springs: NavPress Publishers, 1992), 40.
5. Tan, Electronic Edition: *Encyclopedia of 7,700 Illustrations.*
6. Jones, *1,000 Illustrations*, 342.

### *Chapter 9: You Look Funny!*

1. Frank S. Mead, *12,000 Religious Quotations* (Grand Rapids: Baker Book House, 1990), 430.
2. W. Harris, *The Preacher's Homiletic Commentary* (Grand Rapids: Baker Book House, 1996), 522.
3. Hewitt, *Illustrations Unlimited*, 283.
4. *The Interpreter's Bible: Psalms and Proverbs* (New York: Abingdon Press, 1955), 884.
5. Hewitt, *Illustrations Unlimited*, 283.
6. Gilbert, ed., *Bits & Pieces*, 15 August 1998, p. 4–6.

### *Chapter 10: Can You Handle Success?*

1. Gilbert, ed., *The Best of Bits & Pieces*, 177–78.
2. Mead, *12,000 Religious Quotations*, 430–31.
3. E. C. McKenzie, *14,000 Quips and Quotes* (Grand Rapids: Baker Book House, 1980), 483.
4. Gilbert, ed., *The Best of Bits & Pieces*, 178.
5. Hewitt, *Illustrations Unlimited*, 454.
6. Craig Brian Larson, *Contemporary Illustrations for Preachers, Teachers and Writers* (Grand Rapids: Baker Book House, 1996), 110.

## ALSO BY DAVID IRELAND

### What Color is Your God?

While shopping at a local supermarket one evening, David Ireland is stopped in his tracks when he suddenly notices all the different races of people brought together by their common need for food. At that moment, the Holy Spirit impressed this question upon his mind, "Why can't it be like this in My church?" Teary-eyed and choked up from hearing God's desire to see people model a lifestyle of diversity, a vision for cross-cultural ministry was ignited in his heart. *What Color is Your God?* will enable you to make the emotional shift from leading an exclusively ethno-centric life to becoming wholeheartedly Christ-centered and culturally inclusive.

ISBN: 0-9627907-3-7

$13.00 — soft cover; over 180 pages

### Activating the Gifts of the Holy Spirit

God wants the gifts He has given you to become evident in every area of your life. In this dynamic book, David Ireland shows how you can activate the power of the Holy Spirit in your daily walk with God. Discover how you can...

- Understand the gifts of the Spirit
- Hear the voice of the Holy Spirit
- Know God's heart in every spiritual matter
- Be miraculously used by God
- Take authority over Satan's tricks and deceptions...and more!

ISBN: 0-88368-484-5

$11.00 — soft cover; 175 pages

# Life-Changing Messages Available on Cassette

## 6 Habits of World-Class Leaders

In a rapidly changing world, there is a pressing need for effective leaders. Through this vital, motivational tool, David Ireland describes the habits of world–class leaders and how they use these tools to remain effective in their areas of influence. Through this six-cassette album you will learn such essential leadership skills as:

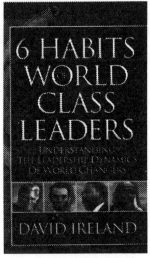

- Failure Gives You an Edge
- How to Develop the Leader Within
- The Importance of Mentoring
- Problem-Solving...and more!

6-Cassettes — $30.00

---

## Understanding Dreams

Throughout the ages, the subject of dreams has mystified scientists and baffled the common man. Yet almost everyone dreams. The Bible proves that these night visions are often used by God to communicate to people in a unique and unobstructed way. Through this revealing three-tape series, Pastor Ireland demystifies the ethereal realm of dreams and shows you how they can provide direction for your life through this provocative, in-depth study.

3-Cassettes — $15.00

# Life-Changing Messages Available on Cassette

## Becoming a World Changer

Every person can effect change in his or her sphere of influence. World changers continually model God's inclusive integrity by reconciling themselves to others of different racial, ethnic, and cultural backgrounds. These courageous men and women refuse to be deterred from their goal to see racial divisions come down. World changers recognize that the reconciliation of man to God is incomplete without the adjoining reconciliation of man to man. Through this dynamic series on three cassettes David Ireland challenges you to reshape your world to enhance the glorious mosaic of God, one life at a time.

3-Cassettes — $15.00

## Home Improvement

In this provocative family series, Pastor David Ireland presents six practical messages outlining practical, biblical principles that will help you strengthen the relationships that mean the most to you. This essential cassette series addresses such complex family issues as:

- Building an Affair-Proof Marriage
- The Blended Family
- Single and Satisfied
- What I Wish My Parents Knew

6-Cassettes — $30.00

## Avoiding Sexual Pitfalls

Judging from today's talk shows, multitudes of men, women, and children have fallen into the disillusioning trap of sexual perversion. In this healing and candid three-tape series, Pastor Ireland exposes the unforeseen pitfalls of sexual sins. Through these messages, he teaches that God never intended sex to be used as a lethal weapon or as a deceptive lure. Rather, God created sex for our procreation and for our pleasure. Learn to put healthy boundaries around your sexual behavior through these practical messages.

3-Cassettes — $15.00

# Life-Changing Messages Available on Cassette

## The Ministry of Reconciliation

The ministry of reconciliation transcends the mere act of soul winning. The church has the additional responsibility to reflect God's restorative nature in producing social harmony based on forgiveness, acceptance, and love of all people. It has been said that 11:00 a.m. on Sunday mornings is the most racially segregated hour in America. This statement leads us to conclude that our theology is sullied by separatism and ethnocentrism. Through this three-cassette series you will discover how God seeks to elevate His church to a place where it embraces and celebrates people of all races, cultures and nationalities.

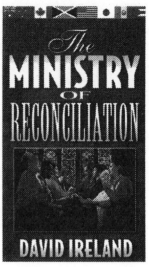

3-Cassettes — $15.00

## Healing Victims of Abuse

This dynamic series offers therapeutic comfort to victims and victimizers of physical, sexual, and spiritual abuse in three cassettes. David Ireland uses his unique expository preaching style to build a bridge of trust for the hurting. In this life-transforming series, our teacher outlines the stages of emotional suffering and maps out a plan that moves the listeners from pain to peace.

3-Cassettes — $15.00

To order these resources visit our on-line bookstore at www.impactminstry.org. You may also use our convenient Order Form on the last page or call **1-800-850-6522** for credit card orders.

# Order Form
(You may photocopy this form)

|  | Qty. | Price | Total |
|---|---|---|---|
| **BOOKS:** | | | |
| What Color Is Your God? | _____ | $13.00 | _____ |
| Activating The Gifts of The Holy Spirit | _____ | $11.00 | _____ |
| Failure Is Written In Pencil | _____ | $13.00 | _____ |
| **CASSETTE ALBUMS:** | | | |
| Home Improvement | _____ | $30.00 | _____ |
| Avoiding Sexual Pitfalls | _____ | $15.00 | _____ |
| Understanding Dreams | _____ | $15.00 | _____ |
| The Ministry of Reconciliation | _____ | $15.00 | _____ |
| 6 Habits of World Class Leaders | _____ | $30.00 | _____ |
| Becoming A World Changer | _____ | $15.00 | _____ |
| Healing Victums of Abuse | _____ | $15.00 | _____ |
| **Subtotal** | | | _____ |

Postage & Handling:
- Add 10% of Order (minimum of $2.00)  _____
- (Orders outside the U.S. add 20%)  _____
- New Jersey residents add 6% Sales Tax  _____

**Total Enclosed (U.S. funds only)**  _____

## Send payment with order to:

IMPACT Publishing House
68 Church Street
Montclair, NJ 07042

For quantity discounts or credit card orders, call:
**1-800-850-6522**

Name: _____

Address: _____

City: _____ State: _____ Zip: _____

Country: _____

For additional ministry resources from David Ireland visit our online bookstore at: **www.impactministry.org**